IMPROVE YOUR SOCIAL SKILLS

By Daniel Wendler

Contents

Manifesto

I

I believe that you deserve a place to belong.

I believe that you deserve relationships where you can be your whole self, your real self, the self that doesn't have it all figured out, the self that makes mistakes, the self that hates itself sometimes. I believe that you deserve people who will see your whole self and accept you wholeheartedly.

I believe that within you is the spark of the divine, that your screw ups and your baggage do not have the power to define you, that no matter what you think of yourself and no matter the names that others have called you, you are overflowing with beauty and passion and potential.

I believe that it is good that you are alive, and that your life is a gift to the people who love you and to the people who have not met you yet but who will love you one day.

II

I believe that you will find people who will help you believe these things, too.

I believe that you will find people who will know and love all of you, who will know your scars and help in your healing, who will count their relationship with you as one of their most treasured gifts.

I believe that you will find people who will see tremendous beauty in you.

I believe they will help you see it too.

Manifesto

III

I believe that you will see tremendous beauty in others, and help them see it too.

I believe that you will speak the words that will encourage someone not to give up, give the smile that will break through someone's dark mood, be the shoulder for someone who desperately needs a safe place to cry.

I believe you will love people so much it hurts, and you will help the people you love discover the best of who they are.

I believe that you will seek the lonely and outcast and be a true friend to them.

IV

I believe that everyone is worth fighting for (including you.) I believe we were made to love ourselves and each other and like warriors we must fight against everything that holds us back from that love.

I wrote *Improve Your Social Skills* because relationships don't happen automatically. Apathy, fear, awkwardness – all conspire to thwart connection. You have to be prepared to fight for your relationships.

So we prepare.

We study. We practice. We train.

Like a swordsman who has mastered his footwork, we learn to move smoothly in conversation. Like a general reads the terrain, we learn to read social cues and nonverbal signals. Like a grizzled veteran, we have made peace with our fear – and we don't let it hold us back from action.

No matter where we start, we can get better. Whether social butterfly or socially awkward, we study, we practice, we train.

Day by day, moment by moment, we learn how to build friendships and how to be a good friend to others. We know our new skills will help us – but more than that, we know that our skills will help us protect others.

When we reach out with love, we protect others from rejection, from shame, from hopelessness. The impact you make can be as small as a smile and as large as a suicide averted.

In love's army, you will be a mighty warrior.

V

I want to live in a world where nobody feels like a reject.

I want to live in a world where nobody stands alone.

I want to live in a world where love and acceptance matter more than success and power.

We don't live in that world, for the most part. But we can help create it.

You can help create it.

Start today.

Introduction

Improve Your Social Skills is a comprehensive, practical guide to social skills. It explains the core principles of social interaction in clear, easy to follow lessons.

I wrote *Improve Your Social Skills* to be the guide I desperately needed during my own social struggles. Growing up, I was the most socially awkward kid you would ever hope to meet. But when I was diagnosed with Asperger's Syndrome in high school, I realized that my social problems were caused by a lack of social skills, not by some inherent flaw in my character.

After my diagnosis, I studied social skills for more than a decade. On January 1st, 2012, I launched ImproveYourSocialSkills.com to share what I'd learned with the world. Hundreds of thousands of people visit the site every year, and today I'm proud to help an even wider audience through the Improve Your Social Skills book.

The guide you're about to read is a compilation of the social principles I've learned during my lifetime of personal social skills study, as well as the techniques I developed while offering hundreds of hours of social skills coaching. It offers detailed blueprints for basic skills like conversation and body language in depth, and provides clear explanations for complex topics like empathy, making friends, and dating.

I wrote *Improve Your Social Skills* to share the principles that have changed my life. These principles led me to a life full of close friendship, satisfying connection, and tender romance. I wrote Improve Your Social Skills because I want everyone to have that kind of life.

I believe you deserve a place to belong. I believe that you can live a life full to the brim with friendship, connection, and love. I wrote *Improve Your Social Skills* to help you believe it, too.

Chapter 1

Foundations

When I was in college, I signed up for an internship with Students International, an organization that works among the poor in the Dominican Republic. I was assigned to the construction outreach where Rudy, the Dominican construction leader, taught me a great deal about both construction and life.

One day, after we'd spent hours painstakingly laying a foundation for a house and making sure everything was perfect, he turned to me and said,

"We always spend more time on the foundation because **the foundation is everything.** If the foundation is solid, the house will be strong. If the foundation is crooked, the house will be flawed. It's the same thing with your life—if the foundation of your life is in solid things, you will be strong. If you set your foundation in crooked things, you will crumble."

(He talked like that ALL the TIME. It was like building houses with Yoda.)

I think Rudy was on to something.

If you take the time to lay your foundation right, then you will be successful in whatever you're building – whether a house, a life, or a set of social skills.

That's what this "Foundations" section is about. I wrote it to help you think through the way social skills affect your own life. This guide is a very powerful tool, but before you pick up any tool, you need to know what you're trying to build. I know you are probably eager to get started on the "meat" of the guide, but trust me (or, if you prefer, trust Rudy.)

The foundation must come first.

Foundations contains four lessons:

- **How to Use the Guide**

  Here are some guidelines to help you get the most out of the guide

- **Setting Goals For Your Social Skills Journey**

  Why are you trying to learn social skills? What are your goals? What has your history with social skills been? Where are you, and where are you going?

- **Overcoming Fear And Social Anxiety**

  Social interaction can be scary, and it's easy for fear to hold us back. But it is possible to overcome your fear, and in this section I show you how.

- **Manipulation vs. True Intimacy**

  Some other social skills gurus recommend using social skills to manipulate others into doing what you want. But truly fulfilling relationships are built on trust and respect, not manipulation and deceit.

How to Use the Guide

You may use the guide however you see fit. Read the entire thing in one sitting. Skip around to the sections that interest you most. Read it out loud to your cat. The world is truly your oyster.

But if you want to get the most out of the guide, I have some advice for you.

- **Read the guide in order.** The later chapters reference concepts from earlier chapters and cover more advanced topics. It is particularly important to read in order within chapters, since the sections in each chapter build directly on one another. You are welcome to skip around all you like, but if you find that a certain chapter or section doesn't make sense, your best bet is to go back and read what you missed.

- **Practice what you learn**. The only way to learn how to apply the principles in the guide to the real world is, well, to get out and apply them to the real world. So take some time every day to practice. Watch TV with the sound low and study the body language of the actors until you can recognize comfort and discomfort. Strike up a conversation with your coworker and practice maintaining conversational flow. Spend a bit of time at the end of the day to think through your social skills goals. Pick a social skill you want to master, and put in some time every day practicing it. You'll find yourself richly rewarded.

- **Study slowly but consistently**. It's certainly possible to fly through the entire guide in one sitting, but there's a lot of content to take in. Give yourself the chance to really absorb everything you can. I recommend a bit each day, reading a subsection of a chapter or two, and then making sure to practice what you read during the day. If you can't wait to dive in, it's okay to read it all at once – but make sure you go back and reread slowly to catch what you missed.

- **Don't go it alone!** Ask friends, family and mentors to help you with your social skills journey. Your support network can be a great source of advice and encouragement.

- **You should have specific goals in mind** as you work through the guide. Improving your social skills just to improve your social skills is good, but it's hard to stay motivated if you don't have clear goals. Having clear goals allows you to track your progress towards that goal and stay motivated. Try taking a moment when you start or finish each chapter to write down a few new goals that relate to the topic of the chapter.

- **Supplement the guide with other sources**. *Improve Your Social Skills* has a lot of great content, but there are other social skills resources that can build on what you learn in *Improve Your Social Skills*. Even today, I keep an eye out for great social skills books so that I can continue to learn and grow my skills. At ImproveYourSocialSkills.com/best-social-skills-books I've compiled a list of some of the best books on social skills, which is a great place to start.

However you decide to use the guide, remember that **practice** and **persistence** are the two biggest keys to your success. Be diligent to practice the things you learn. If you do, you will be well on your way to social success.

Setting Goals for Your Social Skills Journey

A good friend of mine likes to ask me, "Where are you, and where are you going?"

He asks this because he believes that **life is a journey**. The person you were yesterday is different than the person you will be tomorrow, because the person you were yesterday was not shaped by today's experiences. You will change as you go through life.

It's inevitable.

But how you change is **up to you.**

You will be changed whether you spend your weekend watching TV or helping a family build a home, but it is your choice that determines if you pick up the remote or the hammer. Unfortunately, it's hard to make the decision to change for the better. It's easy to put off a beneficial change until later or to give up as soon as the change becomes difficult.

That's why it's important to know where you are and where you're going. When you don't, it's like trying to make a long journey without a map. You won't have the first idea of how to start, and you won't know if you are drawing closer to your goal or just walking in circles.

But if you understand where you are and where you want to go, then you can draw a map. You can plan for the journey and prepare yourself for the obstacles that you might face along the way. The journey may still be a long one, but you know **you will not give up** because you are focused on your destination.

In social skills, knowing where you are means that you understand your current social strengths and limitations, and you understand how those strengths and limitations affect your life. And knowing where you're going means you have a concrete set of social goals, as well as a plan for reaching those goals.

I have some questions to help you find out where you are and where you're going, and I encourage you to think through them in depth. Let the questions inspire your thinking, and don't worry too much about how you respond to each question. There are no right or wrong answers; the questions are only there to guide your thinking.

Where Are You?

- What are your social strengths? Social strengths are the positive elements you bring to relationships and social interactions. They can be social skills, but they don't have to be. Being loyal to your friends or having a genuine desire to get to know others both count as social strengths, even if they might not be social skills.

- Think about the best relationships in your life. These might be current relationships or relationships from your past. What were those relationships like? What made those relationships so good? How did those relationships affect your life?

- How have you tried to improve your social skills in the past? Have those methods been successful? If so, what made them successful? If not, what would help you be more successful this time around?

- What are the current gaps in your social skills knowledge? What are the elements of social interaction that you don't understand, or that you struggle to do successfully?

- Why did you decide to start reading *Improve Your Social Skills*?

Where Are You Going?

- What are the practical areas of social skills that you want to improve? Practical skills are the "nuts and bolts" of social interaction. They include stuff like making conversations flow smoothly, understanding how other people are feeling, and avoiding needless conflict.

- What are your "short term" goals for social skills? Some examples might be making a new friend, having a fun time at a social event, or deepening your relationship with a specific friend. These are goals that you think could be accomplished in the next few weeks or months.

- What are your long term goals for social skills? Some examples might be having someone you consider a close friend or feeling completely comfortable in social situations.

- Who are the people who can accompany you on your social skills journey? These might be friends, family members, or mentors who can encourage you, act as a sounding board, or provide a safe place to practice your social skills.

- What is your motivation for embarking on this journey of social skills improvement? How can you help yourself stay motivated, even when the journey becomes hard?

I encourage you to write down your answers to these questions and return to them on occasion as you progress through the guide. As your understanding of social skills improves, your understanding of where you are and where you are going will change as well.

Take the time to ask yourself "Where am I, and where am I going?" every so often, and you will make sure that you keep growing in the right direction.

Also, remember that slow growth is still growth. It might take you a long time to accomplish your goals, or even to see clear progress. But don't give up.

Every time you try something new or learn a new skill, you are making progress. Learning social skills is a journey, not a race. The speed at which you accomplish your goals is not important; what's important is that you keep journeying forward.

Overcoming Fear and Social Anxiety

I'll be honest.

Social interaction can be scary.

What if you don't know what to say?

What if you do something awkward and people laugh at you?

What if you get rejected?

Social interaction is supposed to be fun. But when you are struggling with anxiety, it's hard to enjoy spending time with others.

Fortunately, there is a way to overcome your fear. You can't turn off fear entirely, but you can keep it from controlling you.

To do this, you need to understand the difference between **true fear** and **physical fear**.

True Fear vs. Physical Fear

- **True Fear** is a good thing. It's your body's way of warning you about danger. If a bear ambles into your campsite, you will feel a jolt of adrenaline, your heart will start pounding, and your brain will start screaming: THAT IS A BEAR. Because of this fear, you will drop everything else that you're doing and work to protect yourself. Your body uses true fear to keep you safe from real danger.

- **Physical Fear** is when your body activates the fear response even though there is no real danger. When a monster jumps out during a scary movie, you might experience the exact same physical response that the bear in your campsite triggered. The difference is that while a bear can hurt you, special effects cannot.

Your body doesn't understand the difference. But you do. You can enjoy a scary movie because you know the difference between a harmless movie monster and the real danger of a bear. And you can enjoy social interactions by learning to distinguish between physical fear and true fear.

Think about it for a minute.

Your fear in social interactions is almost purely physical fear, not true fear. You might be afraid that you will do or say something awkward, or that others won't like you, or that others might judge you. But you know what? Probably none of those things will happen. And even if that does happens, it's ok.

Say it with me. *It's ok.*

Social Anxiety = Physical Fear

If you're talking with someone and say something incredibly awkward, what will happen? Well, you'll feel embarrassed. The other person might become upset, or they might laugh at you. But then you'll recover.

The conversation will move onto a different topic. The other person will forgive your awkwardness and will soon forget it entirely. Worst case, you will try again in a new conversation with someone else.

No real harm is done. Nobody was mauled by a bear.

Social interaction is supposed to be fun, and failure is not a big deal. Read that again. **Failure is not a big deal.** If you mess up in one social interaction, no permanent harm will be done. Take a deep breath, remind yourself that nobody was mauled by a bear, and go strike up a conversation with someone new.

Now, there is an exception to this rule. If you do something to upset or offend someone with whom you have a long-term relationship (like a longtime friend or a coworker), then there may in fact be real consequences since you might damage the relationship. But you have to seriously upset or offend someone in order to cause lasting damage, and if you are making an effort to be sensitive to their feelings, that is unlikely to happen.

Plus, normally your greatest anxiety is not caused by the people that are close to you; it's caused by people you don't know very well. When you don't know someone well, there is no relationship to damage and therefore no real danger.

Freedom from Fear

So next time you feel your anxiety peaking at the thought of a social interaction, remind yourself that it's only physical fear. Social interaction can't really hurt you (even if you make a mistake.)

I know this reminder won't make the physical fear go away. Your heart might still race and your palms might still sweat. But you will have the courage to face down that fear.

Of course, overcoming fear is a process. Your fear might be extremely powerful, especially if you have social anxiety disorder or if you have experienced painful bullying and rejection. And if that's the case, it's ok. I don't expect anyone to read this lesson and instantly banish fear.

Instead, I hope this lesson encourages you to take small but steady steps away from fear. Find a goal that seems scary but doable, and use your knowledge of true fear and physical fear to help you accomplish that goal.

Don't worry if the first time you attempt the goal you fail – remember, failure is not a big deal. And don't feel that you have to accomplish this on your own. If possible, ask family and friends to support you or find a support group to help you on your journey.

(I also recommend that you consider seeing a professional counselor. As I mention elsewhere, counselors can be incredibly helpful, and there is no shame in talking to one. If you're really hurting and you need to talk to someone right now, just call 1-800-442-HOPE and you will be connected to a volunteer counselor.)

The important thing to remember is that anxiety is something you can overcome. It will take time, and it may take the support of friends, counselors, and loved ones, but **you can overcome anxiety.**

Just take small steady steps towards your goal, and remember that no matter what physical fear might want you to believe, **you don't need to fear failure.**

Be courageous.

Manipulation vs. True Intimacy

So, a word on what I'm trying to accomplish here (and what I'm not.)

My goal here is to help you have deep, fulfilling, authentic relationships by giving you a solid foundation in social skills. I'm not trying to teach you everything there is to know about social skills or make you into some kind of social superhero. I just want you to have the skills you need to build great relationships.

Thing is, those skills can be used for bad ends. Martin Luther King Jr was a great orator, but so was Hitler. The thought of using social skills to deceive others or to manipulate people into giving you what you want can be very seductive.

And there are lots of social skills "gurus" out there who teach a message of manipulation and deceit. They claim to teach social skills so you can gain power and influence, convince others to do what you want, or seduce women.

These manipulation-based social skills have a lot of practical problems (most of the techniques don't work, or only work in a few limited instances). What's more, they're just plain wrong.

I believe that most people reading this guide are as committed as I am to building relationships on a foundation of trust and respect, not manipulation and deceit. If that's you, then you can safely ignore this section.

But for those who are tempted by thoughts of manipulation, a word of warning.

The Danger of Manipulation

True fulfilling relationships are **ALWAYS built on mutual trust and respect**. If you manipulate someone, you are disrespecting them, and you will destroy their trust in you as soon as they find out. You might be able to get what you want in the short term by using manipulation and deceit, but in the long term **you will always be found out**.

You will never get the true intimacy you're seeking with deceit.

So if you're looking to learn how to influence people to do what you want, or to seduce women, or to create a false impression of who you are to fool others, my program has nothing to offer you.

But here's the thing. You don't need deceit or manipulation. *Improve Your Social Skills* is based on the philosophy that you don't need to change who you are to be liked or accepted. I believe that if you let people get to really know you, incredible friendships are going to happen. You don't have to twist someone's arm or fool them about who you are. You just need to give them the chance to really know you.

It's true that when you don't have good social skills, it's hard to have the interactions that allow others to get to know you. But social skills can be learned (that's what this guide is for!). And when you are no longer held back by a lack of social skills, your true self will shine through.

That's worth working towards. Don't give up, and don't settle.

Chapter 2

Body Language

Relationships are built on communication. I share with you, and you share with me. When we share with each other, we understand each other better – which grows our relationship deeper.

The tricky part is that a lot of communication is non-verbal. I might not use words to tell you if I feel upset with you, but I might physically draw back from you – for instance, by crossing my arms, angling my feet towards the door, or avoiding eye contact. If you don't catch my physical signals, you might not realize that something is wrong until it's too late.

Even if you understand the body language signals other people are sending, you might not realize what your own body is communicating. When your body language is cold and standoffish, people are unlikely to approach you, even if you want them to.

Fortunately, it's easy to make body language a positive part of your interactions. In this section of the guide, I will walk you through the simple, practical principles that will guide you to a great understanding of body language.

Body Language contains five lessons:

- **Comfort and Discomfort: The Only Two Signals You Need**

  Pick up a book on body language, and you'll be confronted with hundreds of pages filled with different body language signals. The hidden meanings of every possible movement, glance, and nose scratch is explained in painstaking detail. It makes for interesting reading, but it's not very practical to memorize hundreds of body language signals.

Fortunately, there's a better way. There's only two major body language signals that you need to know: "Comfort" and "Discomfort." In this lesson, I explain how to use each of these signals in conversation.

- **A Field Guide to Comfort**

There are several body language signals that indicate someone is feeling comfortable. In this lesson, I teach you how to recognize the most common comfort signals and explain how to respond.

- **A Field Guide to Discomfort**

Much like comfort, bodies also have several ways to signal that someone is feeling uncomfortable. In this lesson, I walk you through the most common discomfort signals so you will know when your partner is feeling uncomfortable.

- **Understanding Body Language in Context**

In order to respond appropriately to body language during a social interaction, you need to understand the context of the interaction. This section teaches you how to recognize key signals from context that help you to respond better to body language.

- **Your Body Language**

Understanding the body language of others is extremely useful, but you also need to understand the messages your own body language is sending. It's easy for your body language and your words to send conflicting messages, which is a recipe for misunderstanding. In this lesson, I help you make sure that your body and your words work together.

Comfort/ Discomfort: The Core of Body Language

Body language helps us understand one another.

If you encounter a friend whose body language shows sadness, you know to ask them what's wrong.

If you start to tell a story and your friend's body language shows interest, you know to keep talking.

It's useful stuff.

Unfortunately, body language is very complex. There are hundreds of different signals our body can send, and unless you are Paul Ekman or are willing to put in decades of work, you can't learn them all.

Fortunately, **you don't need to learn them all.**

In fact, there are only two signals you need to learn: "comfort" and "discomfort."

- Comfort signals tell you that the person is feeling good. People give off comfort signals when they like the person they're interacting with, they enjoy their current activity or interaction, and there is nothing troubling them.

- Discomfort signals tell you that something is wrong. People give off discomfort signals when something is bothering them, when they're not feeling happy, or when they are not enjoying their current activity or interaction.

Responding to Comfort and Discomfort

Comfort and discomfort signals are the clues that tell you how your partner is feeling. Once you know how your partner is feeling, you know how to respond.

Here's how it works:

Think of these signals as red light/green light. If you're picking up "I'm feeling comfortable" messages, then you've got a **green light.**

When you get a green light, your job is simply to relax and enjoy the interaction. Keep an eye out in case their body language changes to discomfort, but otherwise, just relax and keep doing whatever you were doing.

If you're reading "I'm not comfortable" signals, then that's a **red light** (or at least, a yellow "caution" light.) When you get a red light, your job is to help your conversation partner feel more comfortable. Try to learn what caused them to feel uncomfortable and see if you can remove the source of the discomfort.

In other words, this is how you use body language in social interactions:

- Look at body language signals to find out if your partner is comfortable or uncomfortable.

- If they're comfortable, then relax.

- If they're uncomfortable, try to find out what's wrong and fix it.

Comfort and Discomfort in Practice

In practice, this is very simple. Let me give you an example.

A few days ago, my friend asked me a question, and I launched into an extremely long-winded answer. Midway through my response, I checked their body language and realized they were giving off several discomfort signals. Oops.

I realized the source of their discomfort was my long-winded answer (they had wanted a short response, not a massive lecture.) I cut my long-winded explanation short and was rewarded with my friend's body language becoming more comfortable.

My friend never told me that they were bored, but their body clearly communicated it to me. Because I knew how to understand their body language, it was easy for me to see their discomfort and realize I needed to cut my answer short.

People communicate comfort and discomfort to you with their bodies all the time. Learn to understand and respond to these body language signals, and it will be much easier for you to have positive interactions.

Of course, in order to respond to body language in this way, you need to be able to notice when someone is signaling that they are comfortable or uncomfortable. You also need to be able to look at the context to understand what is causing your partner to feel comfortable or uncomfortable. Fortunately, we'll cover all of these topics in the next few lessons.

A Field Guide to Comfort

Comfort is a great signal to receive. When you know that your conversation partner is comfortable, you can relax and enjoy the conversation.

People will signal comfort in a variety of ways, the most important of which I've highlighted below. Your goal is to look for patterns in the signals. If someone is truly comfortable, they will send multiple "Comfort" body language signals.

The list below consists of signals that are both common and easy to spot. It's not an exhaustive list of comfort signals, but it is enough for you to be able to reliably detect if someone is comfortable.

Key Comfort Signals

- **Leaning In, Moving Closer, or Turning to Face You**

When someone is comfortable with you or interested in what you're saying, they want to remove distance between the two of you. You can think of it as "If someone FEELS close to me, they want to BE close to me".

Removing distance can take different forms. Sometimes your partner will lean towards you—a good sign! Other times, they'll turn to face you, or physically scoot closer. They might also remove an object that is between the two of you (for instance, setting their dinner plate aside when at a restaurant.)

Feet in particular are a reliable (if subtle) indicator of someone turning towards you. Someone might consciously choose to face you, but most people aren't consciously aware of what their feet are doing. So if someone turns their feet towards you, that's probably a genuine expression of comfort and therefore a very good sign.

- **A Tilted Head or a Head Rested on a Hand**

A tilted head indicates curiosity, whereas resting their head on their hand implies that they're listening intently. Both indicate comfort. If someone is focused on what you're saying, it's very common to see them leaning forward, resting their elbow on a table and their head in their hand.

- **One Leg Tucked Underneath On a Couch (Girls Only)**

This is a girl-only signal, but a very powerful one. If a girl is sitting next to someone she feels comfortable with, she will often tuck one leg underneath her and turn towards that person. If you are on the receiving end of this, count yourself lucky. It means the girl really enjoys being with you.

- **The "I'm Digging This" Smile**

Generally, someone will not be grinning madly throughout an encounter—if they are, you are probably talking with The Joker and should be concerned.

But when people are enjoying themselves, often the corners of their mouth will be turned up slightly. It's subtle, but I call this the "I'm digging this" smile—it shows that people are enjoying whatever's going on. If you're telling a funny story to your friends and you notice this smile, that's a good sign.

- **Physical Touch**

This is a significant indicator of comfort. If someone is feeling comfortable with you, they're much more likely to touch your shoulder to get your attention, or put their hand on your knee when they ask if you're ok, or give you a hug when they greet you.

Physical touch varies a lot by individuals, so don't worry if someone is not touching you physically—they might just not be touchy. But if someone is touching you, you can conclude that they're feeling fairly comfortable with you.

Mastering Body Language

Focusing on comfort and discomfort is considerably easier than trying to memorize every single facet of body language, but it's still a fair amount to swallow all at once.

Fortunately, you don't need to memorize these all at once. I have an exercise for you that will help you break the body language pieces into bite sized chunks for easy memorization.

The exercise is simple:

- Choose one or two signals from the list.

- Turn on the TV to your favorite show. Ideally, your favorite show should be live-action and have a lot of social interaction. If it doesn't, consider watching another show. Reality TV is actually a very good choice, since it's mostly talking.

- Enjoy the show, but look for the signals you chose as the characters interact. Don't be afraid to rewind a scene to get a closer look at a signal. Keep practicing until you feel confident that you could notice the signals in a real interaction.

- Once you feel like you could recognize the signals you chose in a real interaction, pick a few more and start looking for them as well. Eventually, you'll find yourself able to look for all of the signals on the list.

With a little practice, awareness of body language starts to become second nature. Once you know what you're looking for, it's easy to spot patterns of signals and decipher what your partner is feeling.

A Field Guide to Discomfort

Discomfort signals work together with comfort signals to help you manage interactions. When you realize that someone is uncomfortable, you can quickly take action to fix the situation. Once the person is giving off comfort signals again, then you know you have successfully put the conversation back on track.

Like comfort signals, discomfort signals appear in patterns, and are best understood in context. When you see a discomfort signal, think through the other comfort and discomfort signals you have seen, as well as the overall context.

I've compiled a list of the most common discomfort signals. I've picked these particular signals because they're both very common and very easy to spot, making them the perfect place to begin. This is not an exhaustive list, so as you learn additional discomfort signals, feel free to add them to your repertoire. But this list is all that you need to start noticing discomfort signals and using that information in your interactions.

Key Discomfort Signals

- **Neck Touching or Neck Rubbing**

Your neck is home to many nerve endings that, when rubbed, will lower your heart rate and comfort you. When people are uncomfortable, they will unconsciously touch their necks so that these nerves will activate and help to calm them.

Rubbing or stroking on the front or back of the neck is the most common kind of neck touching, but if the person is wearing a necklace or a necktie, they might fiddle with that also.

- **Face Touching or Face Rubbing**

There are also nerve endings in your face, so some people will rub their face to comfort themselves. Look for rubbing the forehead, rubbing the eyes, playing with the hair, rubbing lips—all of these are behaviors people use to calm themselves down. People will also sometimes puff out their cheeks and exhale.

- **Leg Rubbing**

This is where a seated person puts their hands (or hand) palm-down on their legs and slides it towards their knees. Picture someone wiping off sweaty palms on their pants and you've got the idea.

- **Withdrawing or Blocking**

If someone is in conversation and they become uncomfortable with the person or the topic of conversation, they may try to pull back or place objects between themselves and their partner. They might lean away, adjust their chair so that they're not facing the person directly, cross their arms to block their chest, and/or cross their legs so that their knee is between themselves and the other person.

Be careful with this signal, though. Some people might cross their legs or lean back to sit more comfortably, or cross their arms because they're cold. That's why it's important to look at it in context—if you are seeing crossed arms or legs but otherwise positive signals, you are probably okay.

- **Feet Pointed Away**

Feet are extremely powerful indicators of how someone is actually feeling. If someone's feet are pointed away from their conversation partner, that's often a signal that they'd rather exit the conversation. Of course, this only applies if the person could comfortably and naturally point their feet at their partner—if you're sitting next to each other on an airplane, this doesn't apply because it would be very difficult for them to point their feet at you. But if you're standing facing one another, and you see their feet start pointing towards the door, you might want to graciously bring the conversation to a close.

- **The Interruption Hand**

This is not a sign of discomfort so much as an indication that the other person wants to speak. When someone wants to speak, their hand will often jerk upwards—sometimes with their pointer finger raised. The hand will only raise partway before stopping. Essentially what's happening is that the person wants to interject, but they stopped themselves before they actually said anything. Do them a favor and give them a chance to speak.

- **Very Little Eye Contact**

Nobody maintains eye contact all the time, but when they look away they should soon look back to you. If someone is looking everywhere but you, they're probably not comfortable. A simple way of testing this is to say their name in the conversation: for instance "Isn't that right, Carl?" Most people, upon hearing their name, will look at you and hold eye contact for several moments. If someone glances at you when you say their name, then immediately looks away, they may be uncomfortable.

Also, pay attention if someone is repeatedly looking away from you at one specific thing. For instance, if you're talking with someone and they keep glancing over their shoulder at someone else, it might be that they want to talk to that person.

Acting on Discomfort Signals

Of course, it's not enough to just know when someone is uncomfortable. You also need to take action to make them comfortable again. Fortunately, it's easy to know how to make your partner comfortable if you know how.

Understanding Body Language in Context

Let's say you're in a conversation and you notice that your partner has crossed their arms, leaned away from you, and is repeatedly rubbing their face. That's definitely uncomfortable body language. But why is your partner uncomfortable?

Well, they might be uncomfortable because they don't like the conversation topic.

Or they might be uncomfortable because you have food in your teeth and they're not sure if they should tell you.

Or perhaps something is wrong that has nothing to do with you, like an upset stomach.

If you only look at their body language, you won't have enough information to identify the source of their discomfort. Body language will tell you that someone is comfortable or uncomfortable, but it can't tell you why.

That's why you look at the context.

What Is Context?

Looking at context means being aware of three things:

- **The conversation itself.** Did something in the conversation cause your partner to become more or less comfortable? For instance, if your partner's language changed when you asked a specific question, perhaps there is something about that question that made them uncomfortable.

- **The environment the conversation takes place in.** Conversations don't occur in a vacuum (unless you are an astronaut.) Look around the room to see what your partner might be reacting to. An argument at a nearby table, an overly crowded room, or an ex-girlfriend who just entered the party could all be reasons why your partner suddenly became uncomfortable.

- **Your partner's recent experiences.** Your partner's day did not begin when you started talking with them, and the experiences they had prior to your conversation might still be affecting them. For example, if your partner had a rough day at work, they might give off discomfort signals because they are still thinking about their stressful day.

Applying Context

Take the time to look at context, and you will normally identify a few potential causes for your partner's discomfort. Try to remove the discomfort caused by the context, and see if your partner becomes comfortable.

For instance, let's say their body language signaled discomfort when you introduced a controversial topic. Change the topic and see if their body language relaxes. Is there a bad smell in the room? Suggest changing rooms and seeing if they lighten up.

And remember that if you can't deduce the source of their discomfort, it's usually ok to just ask them what's wrong. You don't need to be Sherlock Holmes; it's enough that you made an honest effort to look at the context.

After all, even if you don't know the source of their discomfort, you can still try to make them more comfortable. Offer to fix them their favorite drink, or pick a fun topic to talk about instead of a serious one. It's preferable to know the specific source of their discomfort, but simply being aware that they are uncomfortable goes a long way.

I know that context can seem overwhelming at first. And in honesty, it will take some practice before you become comfortable with both looking at context and also focusing on the conversation. But I think that as you practice, you will find that looking at context is very simple.

In a nutshell, the purpose of looking at context is to **find clues that help you make your partner more comfortable**. When someone's body language tells you that they are uncomfortable, you can look at context to find out why. Then, use that information to help you remove the source of discomfort. Practice looking at context until it becomes natural, and you will have a powerful tool to add to your social skills repertoire.

Of course, body language is not just about your partner's body language, or even your partner's body language combined with context. Your own body language plays a role, too.

Your Body Language

In the previous lessons on body language, you learned how to understand the body language signals of others. If you detect a body language that signals someone is uncomfortable, you know to look for the cause of their discomfort and then try to remove it. If someone signals that they are feeling comfortable, you know that you can relax and enjoy the interaction.

But how do people interpret the body language signals that you give? It's true that only a few people have trained themselves to consciously analyze body language. But even if your conversation partner never consciously thinks about your body language, they will still subconsciously react to it.

For instance, if your body language exhibits warmth and friendliness, your partner is likely to sense that and relax. If your body language demonstrates disinterest or boredom, your partner will think twice before sharing something personal with you.

When Your Body Language and Your Words Don't Agree

Unfortunately, most people don't think about their own body language. They might spend a lot of time thinking of the perfect words to say, without realizing that their body language and their words are sending very different messages.

For example, say you have had a long, hard day, but your friend wants to talk with you about something that they are struggling with. You obviously care about your friend, so you tell them that you want to talk.

But if during the conversation you are yawning, looking at the clock, and leaning back in your chair with your arms crossed, your friend might conclude that you don't really want to talk with them after all.

They storm off, and you are left wondering what you said wrong. (Of course, you didn't say anything wrong—that's the point!)

That's just one example; it's easy to think of other ways your own body language can create misunderstandings. When your words and your body are sending different messages, people will tend to go with the message that your body is sending. If you didn't mean to send that message, trouble ensues.

The Power of Self-Awareness

Fortunately, that trouble is entirely avoidable. Just **be aware** of the messages your body is sending. Your body is going to communicate—that's just part of being human. Take the time to notice what it is communicating, and you can make sure that your body and your words are sending the same message.

Let me be clear. I'm not talking about changing your body language to mask deception – if your words are communicating something untrue, then you should change your words instead of your body language. Relationships built on deception will **never** give you the long-term satisfaction and intimacy that you need.

Instead, focus on presenting a cohesive, genuine message of the thing that is both **true** and **most important**. If you are tired but you care about your friend, the message that is most important is "I care about you," not "I'm tired" (even though both messages are true.) If you are excited to meet someone new but also nervous, the message that is most important is "I am excited to meet you," not "I am nervous."

The message of "I care about you" is more important than the message of "I am very tired" because your commitment to your friend runs deeper than your physical fatigue. The message of "I am excited to meet you" is more important than the message of "I'm feeling nervous" because your desire to make a new friend is greater than your nervousness.

It's ok to make sure your body language communicates the message that is most important. That's not deception; that's just making sure the most important message is communicated well. When you are aware of your own body language, you can be sure that both your words and your body language reflect the message that is the most true.

So take the time to be aware of your own body language. The lists of comfort and discomfort signals are just as useful when you are using them to understand your own body language as when you are analyzing someone else's. Be aware of what your body is communicating, and make the effort to mute discomfort signals and broadcast comfort signals. You'll find that as you match your body language to your words, you will have much greater success in your interactions.

Chapter 3

Conversation

Most conversation advice doesn't help you make conversation.

It's easy to find tips like "Look your partner in the eye" or "Think of conversation topics ahead of time." These tips are helpful, but they don't explain how conversation actually works–it's like saying "Keep your eye on the ball" instead of explaining the rules of baseball.

Of course, you can still enjoy baseball even if you don't understand the rules. But when you struggle during small talk, it's incredibly frustrating – especially if you don't know how to improve.

The good news?

You don't need to be frustrated anymore.

Improve Your Social Skills is a practical, step-by-step guide to social success – and that means it teaches you how conversation actually works.

You'll learn the bedrock principles of conversation and how to apply those principles to make smooth, engaging conversation. Dive in!

- **The Secret of Conversation Flow**

    What makes some conversations flow smoothly, and others sputter or feel awkward? In this section, I explain the principles of "Invitation" and "Inspiration" and how these two principles work together to create smooth, comfortable conversation.

- **Invitation: The Art of Good Questions**

  Invitations help to add structure to a conversation by clearly communicating to your partner when it's their turn to speak and giving them a topic to speak about. In this section, I discuss invitations in depth and teach you how to use them in your conversations. In addition, since most invitations are questions, I explain how to ask good questions and show how you can build rapport with others using questions.

- **Inspiration: The Heartbeat Of Good Conversation**

  It's possible to build a conversation out of nothing but invitations, but there's a better way. Through something I call "inspiration," you can help build conversation that feels more natural and that encourages more sharing and intimacy between you and your partner. This section explains what inspirations are and how they work

- **Inspiration In Practice**

  Once you understand what inspirations are and what they can do for you, you'll be eager to apply them in your everyday conversation. This section gives you the practical, step-by-step guidance you need to do just that

- **Invitation And Inspiration In Harmony**

  After you've learned about invitation and inspiration separately, it's time to discover how they can work together. This section explains how you can use invitation and inspiration in harmony with each other and equips you to use them in real-world conversations.

The Secret of Conversation Flow

Think back to the most enjoyable conversations you've had. Chances are, those conversations moved smoothly from one speaker to the next, and naturally from one topic to another. There was no sense of "What do I say now?" or "Am I supposed to talk next?" You and the other people in the conversation felt free to enjoy spending time with each other instead of worrying about how to make the conversation work.

What made these conversations so special? Well, they all had something called **conversation flow.** Conversation flow happens when conversation is comfortable, effortless, and smooth. It's the way conversations are supposed to work.

Sometimes, conversation flow seems to happen automatically. You and your conversation partner hit it off, and the conversation feels really smooth and comfortable. That's great when it happens, but what do you do when conversations don't flow?

That's where the principle of **invitation and inspiration** comes in. Invitation and inspiration are the key ingredients of smooth, comfortable conversation.

- An **invitation** is when you say something that explicitly lets your partner know it is their turn to speak.

- An **inspiration** is when you say something that makes your partner want to speak unbidden.

Both serve to prompt a response from your conversation partner and keep the conversation flowing.

These two ingredients create the sense of conversation flow. Learn how to include them in your conversations and you will invite conversation flow into all of your interactions.

With a bit of practice, you will find that invitation and inspiration enable you to build enjoyable, comfortable conversation in all of your interactions. No awkward pauses, forced segues, or fakey small talk.

The Deli Metaphor

Imagine that you and your conversation partner are working in a (poorly designed) deli. Half of the ingredients are at one end of the deli counter, and half of the ingredients are at the opposite end. The two of you need to make a sandwich, so you decide to stand at opposite ends of the counter and slide the sandwich back and forth.

Your partner adds some lettuce, then slides it down for you. You add some mayo, then you slide it back so he can add some turkey. It's a bit of a strange image, but stay with me. This is an extremely useful metaphor.

Now, let's make the image a little stranger. Let's say that you and your partner are chatting as you work (normal enough), but that the sandwich you are making represents your conversation (not so normal.)

You ask,, "How was your weekend?" and slide the sandwich down the counter.

Your partner replies "Oh, it was great. How was yours?" and slides the sandwich back.

You reply "It was fine." and try to return the sandwich. The sandwich travels six inches and stops dead.

What happened? Well, you didn't give your partner a clear **invitation** or a strong **inspiration**. Without either of those things, your partner didn't know what to say next (and perhaps was unsure if it was his turn to speak.) So he didn't respond. The conversation lapsed, and the sandwich stopped sliding.

Remember, an **invitation** is when you say something that explicitly lets your partner know it is their turn to speak. And an **inspiration** is when you say something that makes your partner want to speak unbidden. Without an invitation or an inspiration, your partner might not know what to say or whether to respond. That's why you want to be deliberate to offer invitations and inspirations to your partner.

<u>Invitation: The Art of Good Questions</u>

Remember, our goal is conversation flow. Conversations flow when they move from topic to topic and speaker to speaker in a way that feels smooth and natural. One of your primary tools for helping conversations flow is the idea of **invitation.** An invitation is something you say that:

- Communicates very clearly that it is now your partner's turn to talk, and

- Gives a strong suggestion for what your partner should talk about.

For instance, "What did you do today?" is an invitation. It's obvious that you are inviting your partner to speak, and you are giving a clear idea for what they should talk about (their day!)

Invitations are a foolproof safety net for rough spots in the conversation. If you're not sure what to say next, just throw out an invitation and the conversation will keep going. It's ideal if your invitations relate to something that's already been discussed, but that's not essential (especially if the conversation has halted.) Just throw out an invitation and get the conversation rolling again!

Most invitations are questions, but not all questions are good invitations. For a question to be a good invitation, it needs to satisfy the first two rules I listed above, and it also needs to be open-ended.

The Power of Good Questions

By "open-ended question," I mean an invitation that allows your partner to talk at length, instead of being limited to a short answer. When you ask a closed-ended question like, "Did you have a good weekend?" your partner will likely answer "Yes" or "No." Since you're looking for smooth, flowing conversation, a one-word response is not ideal.

But if you ask the same question in an open-ended way, you will give your partner a much better invitation. When you ask, "What did you do this weekend?" your partner is free to tell you the full story of their weekend. You're still asking about their weekend, but you're asking it in a way that invites them to share.

When you invite your partner to share in this way, something powerful happens. Not only does inviting your partner to share help the conversation to flow, but it also gives you an opportunity to show your partner that **you are interested in them**.

When you ask your partner insightful questions about themselves, it tells them that you want to get to know them better. After all, if you didn't, why would you be asking the questions? The classic writing rule of "Show; don't tell" applies to conversation, too. When you ask your partner questions about themselves, you're not just telling them you are interested in them – you're showing them that you care.

How to Ask Good Questions

Now, there is an art to asking good, insightful questions. If you ask questions that are very superficial ("Do you think it will rain this week?"), you won't find out much about the other person, and they won't get a clear message that you are interested in them. But if you ask questions that are too intimate ("What is your deepest, darkest secret?") you are likely to make people uncomfortable.

The trick is to start superficial, and then slowly go more intimate while keeping an eye on the other person's comfort level. If you find that they start giving signs of discomfort, then you should ask less intimate questions. But if they are giving you consistent signals of comfort, then you can consider that a green light to continue digging deeper.

Two quick words of warning about this principle of digging deeper, though:

- First, this progression from superficial to intimate is something that happens over the course of a relationship, not over the course of one conversation. When you first meet someone, it's appropriate to go from talking about the weather (very superficial) to talking about where they work (a bit more intimate.) It's probably not appropriate to go from talking about the weather to talking about (for example) their painful divorce.

  However, as time goes by and you have more conversations with this person, each conversation is an opportunity to dig a little deeper. Eventually you might get to a place where they are comfortable sharing very intimate things with you, but that will usually happen after you have shared many conversations together.

- Second, if you ask the other person more intimate questions, you should share more intimate things about yourself. If the other person is opening up to you but you are not opening up to them, they will quickly become uncomfortable.

Invitation and Inspiration

Obviously, invitations are really useful. They can protect your conversations from grinding to a halt, and they are a powerful tool for building intimacy and rapport with your conversation partner.

However, as handy as invitations are, you can't build an entire conversation out of them. If the entire conversation consists of explicit invitations, it will feel awkward – like an interview instead of a conversation. Natural-feeling conversation flows from one speaker to the next, sometimes with explicit invitations, but often not. Maintaining conversation flow without relying on invitations is where inspiration comes in.

Inspiration: The Heartbeat of Good Conversation

When conversations flow smoothly, people feel comfortable sharing even without an invitation. They'll chime in whenever they have something they want to share and feel encouraged to share it.

This means that in order to create conversational flow, you should:

- Make your partner comfortable

- Inspire your partner to want to share

Making your partner comfortable is pretty straightforward. Be friendly, pay attention to their body language, and give good invitations so they know you really want to know them better.

But what do I mean by inspiring your partner?

Well, picture two artists taking turns while painting together. The first artist might tell the second artist, "Hey, why don't you put some blue here?" and the second artist might respond with "Ok, then you should put some yellow over there."

That's an invitation, and you can certainly make a painting (or a conversation!) using nothing but invitations.

But there's a better way.

The Beauty of Inspiration

Image that the first artist paints a bold streak of yellow on the canvas. The intensity of the yellow inspires the second artist to create a contrast by adding a somber blue, which in turn inspires the first artist to use shading to highlight the relationship between the blue and yellow, which in turn inspires the second artist to add a new color, and so on until the painting is complete.

That's a painting I would want to see.

A painting created by inspiration building on inspiration will be far more creative and emotive than a painting created by trading invitations.

More importantly, the artists undoubtedly had much more fun (and felt much closer to one another) when they painted in this style.

Inspiration in Conversation

That same effect is true in conversation. When you and your partner inspire each other to share, the conversation flows smoothly and you feel closer one to one another.

In a nutshell, you inspire me when **something that you share makes me want to share something, too.** Notice the word "want" in that definition. Inspiration does not make your partner feel obligated to share. It makes them **want** to share.

This is different from an invitation, because an invitation explicitly tells your partner, "Now is the time to speak – and by the way, this is what you should speak about."

By contrast, an inspiration is much less explicit.

When you inspire your partner, you create a welcoming space where they are encouraged to share but are not required to. Inspiration also gives your partner much more freedom in how they respond. If you ask me, "How was your weekend?" (an invitation), I can only respond by answering your question. But if you tell me a story from the bowling game you went to last weekend (an inspiration), then I can choose how I respond.

I might ask you a question about the game, or share a story from my own weekend, or give my opinion about bowling leagues. It's up to me.

And that means it's not up to you.

When you weave inspiration into your conversations, you can free yourself from the responsibility of knowing what to say next. Inspiration encourages you and your partner to create a conversation together, trusting that the dash of green that you are painting now will inspire me when it comes time for me to put my own brush to the canvas.

You don't need to have an endless list of questions ready, or memorize funny anecdotes that you can share at a moment's notice. You just need to be genuine in what you share, and share it in a way that encourages your partner to share, too.

Inspiration in Practice

It's simple and easy to apply inspiration in your conversations.

When you want to inspire your partner, be deliberate to share something that might inspire them to share their **curiosity**, their **thoughts**, or their **story**.

These are not the only three ways to inspire your partner—anything that encourages your partner to share is an inspiration. But these three ways are effective and easy to learn, so I recommend you focus on them while you're practicing inspiration.

Let's look at each in turn:

Inspire Them to Share Their Curiosity

To inspire your partner to share their curiosity, share something they want to know more about. Use your knowledge of the other person to guide you as you craft great inspirations.

For instance, I'm a big fan of the singer Hayley Westenra. If you tell me that you saw her in concert, you will certainly inspire my curiosity – I'll want to know what songs she sang, how long you've been a fan, and what you thought of the concert. But mention the concert to someone who is not a fan, and you might just get a blank stare.

Fortunately, your inspirations don't have to be perfectly matched to the other person. Just make an honest effort to think about what the other person would be interested in, and you will usually end up ok.

Inspire Them to Share Their Thoughts

When you share your thoughts, it encourages your partner to share their own. Thoughts can be your opinions, your speculations, or a topic that you're curious about.

Be careful about this, though. If you sound like you're lecturing when you share your thoughts, or you belittle people who disagree with you, your partner will not feel comfortable to share their own thoughts. Do your best to share your thoughts in a way that welcomes discussion and different opinions.

If you have trusted friends or family members, ask them for honest feedback on how well you welcome the thoughts and opinions of others. It's possible that you feel very open to the opinions of others, but you are unconsciously doing something that causes others to feel uncomfortable. When you ask family and friends to help you, it's easy to find and fix these unconscious mistakes.

Inspire Them to Share Their Story

By story, I mean the story of their life: the experiences that made them the person they are. This can be big things like marriage and graduation, or little things like a crazy road trip that they did with their friends in high school. These experiences made your partner who they are, and when they share their experiences with you, you will get to know them much better.

The best way to inspire your partner to share their story is to share your own story. Tell them about your years in high school, and they will probably answer with a story from their school days. Tell them about your trip to Europe, and they will probably regale with the story of their visit to Mexico. Tell them about a rough time you went through last year, and they might share some of their own struggles with you.

Sharing your story doesn't have to mean talking about specific events. You can talk about how much you've always loved art, or talk about how a particular fear has always been a struggle for you. The important thing about sharing your story is that you're sharing something that's real and that helps your partner know you better.

In other words, talking about how your identity as a Trekkie has shaped you counts as sharing your story. Talking about why Captain Kirk could totally beat up Han Solo does not count as your story (because you're not talking about you!)

Also, remember that the same rules for intimacy that we previously discussed apply here, too. If you just met someone, you probably shouldn't share a really private part of your story. Give the relationship time to grow, and over time you can share more and more intimate parts of your story.

A Final Word on Inspiration

One more thing. Inspiration is powerful, but it's not an exact science. You might share an opinion with your partner in hopes of inspiring them to share their thoughts, but they respond with curiosity—or a piece of their story. That's totally okay. Your goal is to encourage your partner to share. What they choose to share is up to them.

Make sense?

Awesome. Now that you've been introduced to both invitation and inspiration, let's take a look at how they work together.

Invitation and Inspiration in Harmony

Now that we've looked at both invitation and inspiration, let's discuss how to use them together.

Great conversations need both invitation and inspiration. A conversation based entirely around invitations can sound like an interview – nothing but questions and answers. And conversations based entirely around inspirations are hard to do – what happens when you attempt to inspire your partner and they don't respond?

The best solution is to move smoothly between invitation and inspiration, depending on the needs of the conversation. Invitations add **guidance and structure** to a conversation, and inspirations add **intimacy and flexibility**.

In general, this means you should start conversations with mostly invitations, and use more inspirations as the conversation progresses. If you find the person is not responding to your inspirations, or the conversation has an awkward pause, then return to using more invitations until the conversation is moving again.

In other words, when more inspiration seems appropriate, use more inspiration – but don't be afraid to throw a few invitations in there (or vice versa.)

You should use invitations more frequently:

- When the conversation begins

- When you don't know the other person very well

- When your partner doesn't seem to know what to say next

And you should use inspiration more frequently:

- After your partner has shared something personal with you

- After your partner has asked you a personal question

- After you've gotten to know your partner better

Moving Between Invitation and Inspiration

You want to start conversations with mostly invitations and then move to mostly inspirations, because this starts with the focus on your partner, not on you.

If you begin your conversation with inspirations, then you're putting the focus first on you. You haven't given your partner any reason to believe that you care about their thoughts, so they're unlikely to respond to your inspiration. Plus, because you've only talked about yourself, your partner might assume that you are self-centered – an outcome best avoided.

But when you start with invitations, the focus is clearly on your partner. Your questions reassure your partner that you are interested in them and want to hear their thoughts, so your partner will feel comfortable chiming in when you eventually give them an inspiration.

Now, once you know someone well, you don't need to worry about this as much. If your conversation partner is a close friend, they'll already know that they can respond to your inspirations. Your friendship lets them know that you care about them and their thoughts, which makes invitations less important. But as a general rule, it's always safe to start with more invitations and move to more inspirations.

Sound good? Ok, back to the deli. (You remember the deli metaphor, right?)

The Deli, Day 2

It's another day in the magical deli where your sandwich represents your conversation. You ask, "How was your weekend?" and slide the sandwich down the counter. This is a clear invitation, so your partner knows what to say.

Sure enough, your partner replies "Oh, it was great. How was yours?" and slides the sandwich back. Another clear invitation. You and your partner are doing a great job of starting the conversation with invitations to show interest in each other.

Here's where things get different.

In our first introduction to the deli metaphor, you responded to your partner's question with a flat "It was fine." That killed the conversation and stopped the sandwich. This time, let's see what happens when you try a different response.

Instead of saying, "It was fine", you say:

"Oh, it was great. I just adopted a new dog from the shelter, so we went down to the dog park and played fetch. Then I went to the new Transformers movie with my friends. I didn't really like it, but the special effects were cool."

You slide the sandwich back to your partner, and it zooms down the counter—success!

By now, you know what happened: **Your reply has become a clear inspiration.** Your partner might choose to ask you about your experiences adopting the dog (curiosity), tell you about their favorite game to play with their own dog (sharing their story), or tell you their opinion of Transformers (thoughts.)

Even if you had only mentioned one of those three things, it still would have been a fine inspiration—you don't need to inspire curiosity and thoughts and story-sharing all at the same time. The important thing is that you shared something about yourself, and you created a space where your partner could share something about themselves.

Of course, the sandwich shop is just a metaphor. But the principle of invitation and inspiration works in real life just as well. Combine inspiration with invitation, and you now have the tools to make sure that every one of your conversations flows smoothly and feels natural.

And your instructions for how to use those tools is very simple:

Each time that you speak, either give your partner an explicit invitation to speak, or share something that inspires your partner to share in return.

That's it. That's the core of smooth conversation.

Bonus: Ten Easy Tips for Improving Conversation

1. When you're starting a conversation with someone, reference your social context for your first topic. For instance, if you see someone in class, start the conversation by asking them what they thought of the test you took yesterday. If you see someone at a party, ask them how they know the party's host.

2. Don't let your mouth move faster than your mind. Instead of talking when you're not sure what to say, pause for a moment and collect your thoughts. Nobody will mind a short delay, and when you speak, you'll sound much more polished.

3. Get the other person to share stories, not facts. "Where do you work?" is asking them for a fact. "What's it like to work there?" will encourage them to share a story with you.

4. Don't get trapped in a conversation topic when neither you nor the other person is interested. If you can tell that both of you find the conversation uninteresting, segue to a different topic.

5. If a person's torso and feet start to point away from you, they are probably ready to leave the conversation (even if their head is still pointing to you.) Gracefully bring the conversation to a close. Note: This rule doesn't apply if there is a good reason why their feet and torso should face away from you (e.g. if you are seated in an airplane.)

6. If you're asking multiple open-ended questions and getting only short responses, the other person might feel uncomfortable or bored with the conversation. (For example, if you ask someone, "How was your summer vacation?" and they say, "Ok, I guess," that is a short answer to an open-ended question.) Try changing topics or giving them the opportunity to end the conversation.

7. Give yourself permission to fail. Not every conversation is going to be flawless – I still make social mistakes sometimes, and I teach social skills for a living. Go by the philosophy of "Sometimes you win, and sometimes you learn." In other words, if you mess up in a conversation, don't stress out; just figure out what you can learn from the experience.

8. If you feel your issues with conversation are mostly caused by social anxiety or self-confidence issues, consider seeing a professional counselor. There are very effective therapies for social anxiety and low self-confidence, and the right counselor could really help you.

9. If you ever find yourself at a loss for what to say, try sharing a story from your own life that relates to something from earlier in the conversation.

10. Remember that conversation is a skill like any other. If you practice at it a little every day, you'll get much better over time. Consider setting yourself a goal to do one thing to improve your conversation skills every day – perhaps reading a conversation book, talking to a friend, or going to a social event.

Chapter 4

Group Conversation

In the previous section on conversation, I laid out a detailed blueprint for conversation. I explained how to build conversations that flow smoothly, feel comfortable, and lay the foundation for great relationships.

However, most social interaction takes place in a group setting, and navigating the waters of group conversation can be much trickier than one-on-one conversations.

Trickier, that is, until you know the principles behind group conversations and joining groups. And as luck would have it, those principles are what we'll discuss next.

Group Conversation contains three lessons:

- ## Open and Closed Groups

  In order to successfully join a group at a social event, it's important to make sure the group is welcoming to new members. If you know how to read a group's body language, it's easy to discern whether a group is open or closed to new members. In this lesson, I teach you the key signals that show a group is open to your approach.

- ## Joining Group Conversation

  Once you've identified a welcoming group, you need to walk up and start participating in the conversation. That's easier said than done, so this lesson teaches you the practical techniques you need to join new groups and participate in group conversations.

• Group Conversation Flow

Once you've begun participating in a group conversation, how do you make sure that the conversation continues to flow smoothly? And how do you speak up in conversations where you feel uncomfortable or on the outskirts? This lesson has the answers.

<u>Open and Closed Groups</u>

In the next few lessons, we'll discuss how to participate in group conversations.

However, to participate in group conversations, you need to join a group. That can be easier said than done.

I've often walked into a social event, only to find everyone already bunched up in small groups. Nobody waves to invite me into their group, and I don't see any other solitary newcomers to cling to.

You've probably been there, too, and standing alone is a real bummer. What do you do?

Well, first of all, don't panic.

Second, take a moment to scan the room for a group to join. You want to quickly categorize groups into **open groups** and **closed groups**.

Open groups and closed groups are exactly what they sound like. Open groups are open to new people joining them, while closed groups are not open to newcomers.

Closed Groups

You can normally tell whether a group is open or closed by looking at their body language. For instance, a closed group will close off from the crowd—they will move closer together, plug the gaps in between members of the group, and turn directly towards each other.

Closed groups are not necessarily unfriendly, and a group that is closed now might become open later. When a group is closed, all it means is that they are content with the number of people currently in the conversation, and they're not interested in more people joining. They might be closed because they are discussing a sensitive topic, or simply because they don't want to go through the rigmarole of welcoming a new person to the group.

People rarely make a conscious decision to close off their group; the closed signals that you see are their body language communicating their desire to be left alone. Respect the signal their body language is sending, and focus instead on open groups.

Open Groups

Open groups are groups that don't mind new people joining them. They have a "the more the merrier" mindset, and people might flow in and out of these groups naturally. These are the groups you want to target.

The easiest way to find open groups is by looking at body language. Open body language will look different depending on how many people are in a group, so let's examine the different ways groups will show their openness.

One Person

Open and closed is not limited to groups – individuals can also be open and closed. One open person will be **facing the crowd and not busy.** Look for full facings—their feet, torso and face all pointed towards the center of the room or towards the crowd. They will look alert and excited, and ready for someone to come over.

In contrast, closed individuals will be looking down, facing towards the door, or otherwise orienting themselves away from the group. It's common to also see them busy with an activity – reading a book, texting, etc.

However, it's possible that individuals that might look closed would actually love to be approached, but instead close themselves off because they feel shy or uncomfortable. Because of this, it's usually fine to approach a closed individual **as long as you are cautious**. Keep an eye on their body language, and be ready to gracefully exit the conversation if you sense they would rather not talk.

In other words, if they light up when you say hello and you see their body language becoming more comfortable, then you have a green light to keep chatting. On the other hand, if their body language remains uncomfortable or they act standoffish and cold, it's best for you to excuse yourself.

Two or Three People

For a pair or trio of people talking, look at **how they face one another.** If group members are facing directly towards each other, they are more likely to be closed. In contrast, if group members are angled away from one another, they might be happy to have you join their group.

To determine where someone is facing, pay attention to where their feet, torso, and face are pointed. It's common to find two people whose faces are pointed at each other, but whose feet and torsos are facing the crowd. The more of those three factors (feet, torso, and face) are pointed away from other group members, the stronger the indication that you would be welcome to join their group.

Large Groups

For large groups, pay attention to the **shape of the group.** Open groups have gaps large enough for you to walk through. Look for something like a horseshoe shape – the gap in the horseshoe is where you can stand to enter the conversation. Groups with no large gaps between their members are closed off, and you will have a difficult time breaking into them.

Also, keep an eye out for large groups formed around **public spaces**. By public spaces, I mean an area or activity at a social event that everyone is welcome to join. If you're at a Superbowl party, the TV is a public space. If you're camping, sitting around the fire is a public space. Groups formed around a public space are almost always open groups, and it will usually be socially acceptable to join them.

Joining a Group

When you know how to read open and closed body language, finding the right group to join is easy. Just make sure that you continue to pay attention to body language once you've joined a group. If the group turns away from you or otherwise closes off, perhaps they were not open after all, and you should seek greener pastures. In most cases, though, the group will stay open or turn towards you—if that happens, you can relax and enjoy the conversation.

Of course, it's hard to enjoy the conversation if you are only a listener. It's one thing to join a group conversation, and another to be a full participant. Fortunately, with a little practice you'll find it easy to jump into group conversations!

Joining Group Conversations

Knowledge of open and closed groups will guide you towards the best conversational groups to join, but you still have to actually join a group. Simply standing near an open group does you no good; your goal is to become a full member of the conversation.

It's possible that someone else will invite you into a group without any effort on your part, but it's best not to leave things to chance. Once you've approached a group, you need to be deliberate to integrate yourself into the conversation.

Fortunately, integrating yourself into a conversation is easy when you know how. You have two options for integrating in a group – the direct approach and the indirect approach.

The Direct Approach

The direct approach is simple and straightforward.

Walk up to the group and wait for a brief pause in the conversation or for attention to turn to you. Then, introduce yourself and immediately ask a follow-up question.

The trick here is to have a question to ask immediately after the introductions. If you walk up and introduce yourself, then just stand there, that's awkward. But if you introduce yourself and then ask an engaging question, you're off to a good start.

Two things to keep in mind with this question, though:

- **First, make sure your opening question relates to the context.**

If you don't reference the context, your question can seem weird or awkward. But if you reference the context, people are much more likely to accept your question.

By context, I mean the environment around you, as well as the information the person is displaying about themselves. If you're at a party, the party is the environmental context, so you can ask questions like, "How are you enjoying the party?" or "Have you tried the chocolate fondue fountain yet?"

You can also look at the information the person is displaying about themselves – for instance, the things the person is wearing or the activities the person is participating in. If someone is wearing a Darth Vader shirt, you could mention their shirt and ask them if they are a Star Wars fan. If someone sang a karaoke song, you could ask them where they learned to sing.

Just make sure that it's clear what you're referencing. If someone is wearing a Darth Vader shirt but you don't make any mention of the shirt when you ask them about Star Wars, they might be confused by your question. Otherwise, it's pretty easy to use the context in your opening question.

- **Second, make sure your opening question is open-ended and engaging**.

I discuss open-ended questions at length in the section on invitation, so I won't repeat myself here. But if you're fuzzy on how to ask a good question, make sure you read that section and refresh your memory before jumping into conversations. Remember, your goal with the direct approach is to get a conversation rolling, and you can't do that with a closed-ended question.

Of course, it's not always easy to just walk up and introduce yourself. For the times where a more subtle method is needed, you can apply the indirect approach.

The Indirect Approach

The direct approach requires you to interrupt whatever the group was previously discussing, and redirect the conversation towards whatever your opening question was. With the indirect approach, you join in with the group's existing discussion. Both approaches are perfectly valid, so feel free to try both.

You have a few different options for making an indirect approach:

- **Join a group that includes someone you know.**

This is the easiest option. When you join the group circle, make eye contact with your friend and greet them in some way (wave, nod, say hello). The goal is to both let your friend know that you are there, and to let everyone else in the group know that the two of you are friends. When this happens, your friend will often invite you into the conversation, or someone else in the group will ask your friend to introduce you. Either way, you have successfully joined the conversation.

- **Join the group without announcing yourself, then participate as if you were there all along.**

This can feel awkward at first, but people will usually quickly accept your presence, especially if you're in a context (like a party) where people are moving in and out of groups all the time. It's also more likely to work with larger groups – if there are only two or three people in a group, you probably need to announce yourself when you join.

Also, bear in mind that this method only works with open groups. If a group is displaying closed body language, you can seriously irritate them by wandering into their conversation uninvited, so be careful. If you're not sure whether or not a group is open, it's best to not use this approach.

- **Join by mentioning something you overheard.**

This works best if you are near the group and can listen for a period of time before joining. Just listen until you overhear something that you can comment on, then turn to the group and say something like, "Wait, are you guys talking about the new Switchfoot album? I like their older stuff – do you think I should get the new album?" Don't spend very much time listening for the perfect topic to jump in on. Even if your segue is slightly forced, people will usually accept it.

Enjoying Group Conversation

Once you've joined a conversation, relax and enjoy. Make sure you speak up every now and then, but don't monopolize the conversation (other people want to talk too). Use group conversations as a place to learn more about potential friends. If you connect with someone in a group conversation, try to chat with them later one-on-one and get to know them better.

Of course, there are some principles of group conversation that will help you make the most of those interactions and increase your chances of making a new friend from a group conversation. Our next lesson tells you everything you need to know about smooth flowing group conversation, so keep reading!

Group Conversation Flow

In the previous section on conversation, we discussed how invitation and inspiration work together to help conversations flow. With a little practice, you will find it easy to use invitations or inspirations to avoid awkward pauses and keep the conversation flowing.

These principles can also be adapted to group conversations. Group conversation is tricky, because it forces you to divide your attention among all members of the group. But with a little practice, you'll find group conversation can be just as rewarding and fun as one-on-one conversation

Group Conversation Flow

Conversation flow is just as important in groups as it is in two-person conversation. No matter how many people are participating in a conversation, it's important for the conversation to flow smoothly and feel comfortable.

However, your role in creating conversation flow will be different when there are more people in the conversation.

In two-person conversation, you helped to create flow by ensuring that your partner always wanted to speak once you stopped speaking. But when there are multiple people in the conversation, flow takes a different form. Because there are many participants in the conversation, it's likely there will always be at least one person who is willing to speak up.

This means that inspiration is not as essential. It's still important to share something that inspires others to share as well, but with multiple participants the conversation is likely to continue even if you don't inspire anyone else to share.

Letting Everyone be Heard

However, it's not uncommon for a few speakers to monopolize the conversation, while everyone else in the group simply listens. While on occasion this is ok – sometimes folks just want to listen – it's not good when someone wants to speak but doesn't feel included. That's why it's important to make sure that **every person in the conversation feels invited to speak**.

This means exactly what it sounds like. Periodically, try to make invitations to those who have not spoken much, so they have the opportunity to join the conversation. Ask them a question, or their opinion, or say something like, "Oh yeah, Jack had an experience like that – Jack, why don't you tell us about the time you..." When you do, they will feel encouraged to speak, and later in the conversation they will be more likely to chime in without needing an invitation.

It's doubly important to do this if you notice signs of discomfort from someone who is not speaking. If someone is showing signs of discomfort and is not speaking up, they might feel excluded or wonder if they are really wanted in the conversation group. Dispel their fears by drawing them into the conversation, and you will likely be rewarded by seeing their body language relax.

Now, you don't need to be on constant patrol for people who are not speaking up. Your primary focus should be on enjoying the conversation. But when you notice someone who has fallen silent, extending an invitation to them will keep the conversation flowing.

Plus when you draw someone into a conversation, you make them feel welcome and included. I've experienced being on the outskirts of a group at various times in my life, and I still remember the people who made the special effort to draw me in. When you make an effort to invite people to participate in the conversation, you not only encourage the conversation to flow, but you might spark the beginning of a friendship.

Letting Yourself be Heard

Of course, sometimes you are the one who feels on the outskirts of a group. What do you do in that situation?

Well, there's no one-size-fits-all perfect solution. But in order to find the right solution for you, just follow one simple rule: **Self-examine to see where your feelings of exclusion are coming from**

It's important to know why you feel excluded in a group because the source of those feelings will help determine how you respond to those feelings. Do you feel like you are on the outskirts because nobody in the group is talking with you? Well, perhaps you need to take the first step and be more deliberate to join their conversation.

Do you feel excluded because group members are actively making fun of you and putting you down, or because group members have made it explicitly clear they don't want to spend time with you? Well, chances are the folks in that group are not good friend material anyway. You should cut your losses, leave that group, and spend time with people who will be good friends to you.

Do your feelings of exclusion spring from your own social anxiety rather than the actual behavior of the group members? Perhaps you should spend some time getting in touch with your own feelings, so you can tell when others truly don't want you there or when your sense of exclusion is simply your anxiety talking.

No matter why you feel excluded, you'll find that taking the time to reflect on the source of your feelings makes it easy to develop an appropriate response. And when you know how to respond, you'll be able to negate your feelings of exclusion and enjoy everything group conversation has to offer you. No more being held back by fear or awkwardness. Just you, some soon-to-be-friends, and smooth, enjoyable group conversation. That's a goal work working for.

Chapter 5
Empathy

Empathy is the art of seeing the world as someone else sees it. When you have empathy, it means you can understand what a person is feeling in a given moment and understand why other people's actions made sense to them.

Empathy helps us to communicate our ideas in a way that makes sense to others, and it helps us understand others when they communicate with us. It is one of the foundational building blocks of great social interaction and, quite obviously, powerful stuff.

But how do you get empathy? How do you understand what someone else is feeling, if that isn't happening automatically?

Well, to a certain extent we are all designed to naturally empathize with others. Our brains are wired to experience the emotions that someone else is feeling. That's why we wince when someone hits their hand with a hammer, or why we're more likely to laugh if someone else is laughing too. There's an excellent book called *Social Intelligence* by Daniel Goleman on this topic, which explains all of the research behind this natural empathy.

Unfortunately, only a few people have excellent natural empathy. Our empathic wiring exists on a continuum. Some people have fantastic natural empathy and can pick up on how someone else is feeling just by looking at them. Some people have only a tiny amount of natural empathy, and they won't notice that you are angry until you start yelling. Most people lie somewhere in the middle and understand how someone else is feeling only part of the time.

Fortunately, empathy is part talent and part training. Depending on your starting level of ability, getting better at empathy might require more or less work than someone else – but no matter what your starting point, **you can teach yourself to be better at empathy.**

And this section is here to teach you how.

Empathy contains three lessons:

- ## Understanding Yourself

  If you want to understand the emotions of others, you have to learn to empathize with yourself. *Understanding Yourself* was written to help you understand and accept your emotions. Understanding and accepting your own feelings is essential for a healthy life, and it's the foundation of empathizing with others.

- ## Understanding Others

  Through practice and a commitment to thoughtfulness, anyone can learn to understand how others are thinking and feeling. *Understanding Others* is the blueprint that shows you how.

- ## Nonverbal Empathy

  When you understand what someone else is thinking or feeling, it becomes easier to interact with them. But there's a nonverbal aspect to interaction that deserves special attention. The knowledge you gain from empathy can help you to use appropriate nonverbal communication. *Nonverbal Empathy* explains how.

Understanding Yourself

Learning to empathize with others is a key skill in social interactions. If you understand what other people are thinking and feeling, you'll be able to be a better friend and have better interactions.

However, to learn to empathize with others, you first need to learn to empathize with yourself.

That sounds really touchy-feely, but stick with me. This is important, and incredibly practical. Learning to empathize with yourself means learning to **understand and accept what you're feeling and why you're feeling it**.

If you're feeling angry, you should be able to recognize, "I feel angry," and understand the reasons why you feel angry. You should be ok with feeling your emotions and not ignore them or stifle them.

Fundamentally, if something really bad happened to you, it should be OK that you feel sad. You should give yourself permission to feel sad. Sometimes, we get this idea that we need to act happy all the time, or that our problems are not as important as the problems of others, so we feel selfish when we are sad or upset.

But **that's not true.** Your problems matter, because you matter. And if something is happening to hurt you or make you feel sad, it's ok to express that sadness and to let yourself feel that sadness. You don't have to keep that bottled up.

Accepting Your Emotions

Of course, it's a great idea to try to improve your situation, so whatever is causing you to feel sad isn't causing that sadness anymore. You don't have to STAY sad.

And, although everyone gets sad or angry sometimes, if it seems like you're sad or angry all the time, you should think seriously about seeing a counselor. Just like a doctor can help you heal physically, **a counselor can help you heal emotionally**, and there's no shame in talking to one.

That goes for more than just understanding emotions, by the way. If you're struggling with depression or anxiety or loneliness or any number of other things, see a counselor. There's no shame in it, and it might just change – or save – your life. (If you need to talk to someone right away, call 1-800-442-HOPE and you'll be connected to a volunteer counselor for free.)

But the point is that you should give yourself permission to experience the feelings you have. If something bad happened to you, it's ok that you feel sad. You should feel comfortable telling friends and family what you're feeling, even when you're not feeling positive, or even when you're not sure why you feel the way you do. On a fundamental level, you should accept that your emotions are a part of you, and **just as you need to accept yourself, you need to accept your emotions.**

Take a second and re-read through that paragraph again. No, really. Go back and read it. I'll wait.

Understanding Your Emotions

Ask yourself seriously if these things are true for you. Do you understand the cause of your emotions when you feel something? Do you give yourself permission to feel an emotion? Do you accept that it's ok to feel the way you do? Do you have a healthy way to express those emotions?

If the answer to any of those questions is, "No," or, "I'm not sure," then take some time to think through how you experience emotions. Ask yourself why you are answering in that way, and what you need to do to better empathize with yourself. Talk with someone you trust and get their advice and support, or consider making an appointment with a counselor.

It might take some time to process through this, but **it's worth the investment.** Having a solid and healthy understanding of your own emotions helps you to live a happy, healthy life. Humans are emotional beings, and your emotions are a part of who you are.

And, of course, emotions are a part of everyone else, too. If you understand what it's like when you feel an emotion, you'll be better able to understand and interact with a person who is feeling something similar. So even if you don't want to understand your emotions for your own sake, do it for the sake of your relationships with others. It's worth it.

Thinking It Through

I have an exercise for you to do today. It might seem a little weird, but trust me – I think you'll find a lot of benefit to it.

As you go through the day, keep an eye on your emotions, and look for the times in which you are feeling something (whether that something is frustration or happiness or sadness or boredom or anything else). Then, take the time to **think through why you're feeling that way**.

I want you to go below the surface here. It's easy to have someone cut you off in traffic and say, "Well, I feel angry because I was cut off." But if you think a bit deeper, you might find that you're angry because the other driver disrespected you, and you often don't feel respected in your other relationships. Or, you might feel angry because you're hurting from a hard time that you're going through, but you're not acknowledging that pain. You might even realize you don't have a good reason to be angry, and then your anger fades away.

Think through your emotion in whatever way works best for you. Perhaps you might set aside some time at the end of the day to go for a walk, so you have a quiet time to think. Perhaps you could write down your thoughts on your emotions for the day, and then compare your notes from different days to look for trends. Or perhaps you should ask a friend or family member to help you understand your emotions, and talk it over with them.

Whatever the result, I think you'll find at the end of the day you understand yourself a bit better, which in turn will make it easier for you to understand others. Give it a try. And when you feel you are starting to understand your own emotions, read on to find out how to understand the emotions of others.

Understanding Others

In the last lesson, we talked about how to empathize with yourself. Empathizing with yourself helps you to empathize with others, because if you understand your own feelings it is easier to understand the feelings of others.

However, if you really want to understand others, you need more than self-empathy. You also need to spend some time thinking about the way other people understand the world.

This sounds complicated, but it really boils down to one thing:

Train yourself to ask the question "**How does this situation appear to the other person**?" during **every interaction** – and spend the brain cycles necessary to think of a reasonable answer.

The goal here is not to be a mind reader or to know with certainty what the other person is thinking. All you need to do is imagine what it would be like to be that person, and make some reasonable guesses about what that person is thinking or feeling.

Empathy and the Art of Sock Collection

For instance, let's say a friend corners you and starts chatting about a topic you find excruciatingly boring (their sock collection, perhaps).

If you view the situation from your perspective, you're liable to get frustrated and snap at your friend – they should have known how boring socks are to you!

But if you take the time to look at it from the friend's perspective, **you get a better understanding of their actions**. Most likely, if the person is your friend, they care about you and they're not trying to bore you. Chances are that in their excitement to tell someone about their new alpaca wool crew socks, they just forgot how boring socks are to you.

From your perspective, you have been trapped in a boring conversation. From their perspective, they're sharing something exciting with you.

Once you take the time to look at it from their perspective, **you can handle the situation in a much better way**. You won't snap at them now – you understand that they don't mean to bore you.

Instead, you might try to gently change the subject. Or, you might decide this is an opportunity to grow closer to your friend, and use the conversation to find out more about something (socks!) that is important to them.

The Danger of Your Perspective

Unfortunately, our natural tendency is to see things from our own perspective (that's why it's called OUR perspective.)

Rather than trying to find out how the other person sees things, we try to convince them to see things our way. Instead of accepting that the other person will always see things differently, we get angry at them for not seeing things the same way we do.

I used to be guilty of this all the time. I would do something that my parents found disrespectful, so they would get upset with me. Then, I would get upset with them for being upset with me!

I didn't mean to be disrespectful, so I became indignant when they accused me of disrespect – it seemed like my motives should have been obvious to them!

The Need for Discipline

Everything changed once I started to train myself in empathy, I began to ask myself, "Why are my parents so upset?" And when I really thought through that question, I realized that even though I didn't mean disrespect, my parents still felt disrespected. I have great parents, but they're not mind-readers, and so they couldn't know my motives – only my actions.

Once I realized this, I was much better equipped to handle our conflict in a positive way. I would ask myself, "How would this look to my parents?" when I was considering an action, which helped me avoid saying or doing something that would upset my parents. Our relationship improved, and conflict with my parents became much less common.

I share that example to illustrate a key point. When people do something that seems irrational to you, it **still makes sense from their perspective**. If you take the time to step back and ask, "Ok, why is this person behaving like this?" you will usually find a reasonable answer, and that answer will help you respond better.

But asking that question doesn't happen automatically. **You need to make a deliberate decision** to ask yourself, "How does this look to the other person?" You need to be willing to surrender your insistence that the other person sees things your way. And you need to do this again and again and again, until it becomes automatic.

The Power of True Empathy

Building empathy is not easy. I'll admit that.

But as you continue to ask yourself, "How does this situation appear to the other person?" something remarkable will occur. The question itself will become less and less necessary. You will start to intuitively sense how the other person is feeling.

In other words, **you will start to develop true empathy**.

This does take time. You've spent a long time looking at the world exclusively through your own perspective, so you will have to overwrite many years of habit. But trust me, it's worth it.

Empathy in Practice

I have an exercise for you today, too. You might find it difficult at first, but it will kick-start your ability to build empathy towards others. Here's the exercise:

In the conversations you have today, ask yourself, "What is the other person thinking and feeling right now? How are they perceiving this interaction?" Of course, you won't know for sure if your guess is accurate, but more likely than not, you'll be close.

Once you feel comfortable asking that question, **see if you can act on that knowledge**. Maybe the grocery store clerk says, "Hi," to you in a dull voice, and you realize, "Gosh, this person has probably been working all day, and they're feeling worn out." Well, see if you can cheer them up! Tell them they're doing a great job, compliment them on their smile, or ask them where they got their earrings.

It will take time to become comfortable with this, but it becomes easier each time you do it. Once you learn to develop empathy with others, it will become second nature to show empathy to them.

Nonverbal Empathy

When you ask yourself what other people are thinking and feeling, you gain insight into how best to interact with them. This insight helps you defuse conflict and guide the conversation.

There is a nonverbal element to responding to empathy as well. If you realize a friend is sad but ask them, "What's wrong?" in a very cheerful way, your friend might think you don't really care. But when you change your tone to sound sympathetic and concerned, your friend is more likely to believe you want to hear what's wrong. As you might remember, your words and your nonverbal signals work together to communicate, and you want them to be in harmony.

Now, I realize I've given you a lot to work on already. Empathy will eventually become second nature for you, but it can be a lot of work to train yourself to be aware of what the other person is thinking and feeling. When you add the need to manage your own nonverbal signals, empathy can seem overwhelming.

But don't worry. Nonverbal empathy is actually very simple. Similar to the way that body language boils down to just two signals, there are only two nonverbal empathy options you need to worry about: whether to be high-energy or low-energy.

What do I mean by high-energy and low-energy?

High and Low Energy Defined

When someone is high energy, they tend to act

- Excited

- Expressive

- Loud

In contrast, when someone is low energy, they tend to act

- Reserved

- Relaxed

- Quiet

Note that high-energy doesn't always mean happy, and low-energy doesn't always mean sad. Someone who has just won the lottery might jump up and run around the room celebrating, or they might lean back in their chair with a slow, satisfied smile spreading across their face. Both are happy responses, but one is high-energy and one is low-energy.

Also note that people will feel high-energy sometimes and low-energy other times. When you see your friend in a moment of excitement, you should conclude, "My friend is feeling high-energy right now," rather than decide, "My friend is always high-energy."

Energy and Empathy

The idea of high-energy and low-energy is simple enough. But how does it apply to empathy?

Well, if your partner is high-energy, **try to be high-energy.**

And if your partner is low-energy, **try to be low-energy.**

Here's what I mean by that.

Let's say you meet a friend for dinner. Your friend has had a busy day, and you notice they are less boisterous than usual. They are clearly feeling low-energy.

You, on the other hand, are very excited about the restaurant. So you gush about the food and the ambiance, you flirt with the wait staff, and in general, you act expressive and excited. Your friend, meanwhile, picks at her food and wishes you would settle down, so she could have a quiet conversation with you.

In other words, you are being high-energy, and your friend is being low-energy. Your friend wants a restful evening, while you want to party and be goofy. Because there's a mismatch, it makes it harder for you to connect with your friend.

Nonverbal Energy Matching

But if you match your energy level to your friend's energy level, the evening will go much better. When you notice your friend is low-energy, you can act more reserved and sedated, even if you are feeling excited. Or, if you notice your friend is high-energy, you can respond by acting more expressive and boisterous.

Note that you should match your partner's energy level, not exceed it. If your partner is relaxed and sedate, you should be low-energy, but there's no need to act like Eeyore. If your partner is boisterous and loud, you should be high-energy, but there's no need to go crazy.

Energy matching applies to social situations, too, not just to individuals. For instance, a formal event is likely to be low-energy, (so it's wise to be somber and reserved, even if you feel excited), whereas a party is likely to be high-energy (so it's wise to be more expressive and boisterous, even if you feel relaxed.) When entering a social situation for the first time, take a moment to figure out the energy level of the situation, and then use it to guide your own energy level.

Of course, your own energy level matters, too. If you're feeling high-energy or low-energy, it's ok to express that, even if your partner is feeling something different. But it's wise to start by matching your energy level to your partner, and then move back to your natural energy level. This allows your partner to move energy levels with you.

When you monitor the energy levels of those around you and adjust your own energy level accordingly, you'll find connecting with others to be much easier. Plus, you're also practicing being aware of what others are thinking and feeling, which will feed back into your study of empathy in general.

As you begin to master empathy, you'll find yourself understanding others better, having fewer conflicts, and building better relationships. That's a reward well worth the effort.

Chapter 6

Meeting People

Ok. You've practiced your conversation technique. You've brushed up on body language, and you're starting to train yourself to see things from your partner's perspective. You feel ready to go out and make some friends.

Unfortunately, unless you are five, your Mom is not going to set up play dates for you. The responsibility for meeting people and creating a connection with them falls squarely in your lap.

This is a tough responsibility because it means going outside your comfort zone. Unless you are a natural extrovert, you probably prefer spending time by yourself or with people that you already know. A social event filled with strangers can feel overwhelming and draining.

Fortunately, meeting people is **not as hard as you think**.

Social events don't need to feel like you versus a room full of strangers. When you find a group that fits your personality and interests, it's much easier to feel comfortable and connect with potential friends. Learn how to identify the right groups, and you'll find that meeting people is much easier.

Plus, you don't have to be limited to making friends at social events. Potential connections are all around you – from a classmate sitting next to you to a barista taking your order. Learn to take advantage of the connection opportunities that life sends your way, and you'll find yourself richly rewarded.

In other words, **there are bedrock principles that you can learn to take the guesswork out of meeting people and making new friends**.

That's what this section is all about. Let's dive in.

Meeting People contains three lessons:

- ### Finding Your Group

  Social groups are not created equal. Some groups will make it much easier to make friends than others. In this section, I show you how to find the right group for you.

- ### Everyday Connections

  Social groups are not your only option for meeting new people. In this section, I explain how connecting on a person-to-person level allows you to make friends with the people you meet in your day to day life

- ### Person-to-Person Connections

  When you connect with people on a person-to-person level, you open the door to a new friendship. This lesson builds on the advice in the *Everyday Connections* lesson and gives practical guidelines for connecting with others on a person-to-person level.

<u>Finding Your Group</u>

If you ask someone for advice on meeting new people, they will probably respond, "Go join some social groups."

That's true, but not very helpful. Not all social groups are created equal, and if you join a group that is a poor fit for you, it will be hard to make friends.

Sounds obvious, I know. But **people often miss this.**

Many people sign up for groups willy-nilly, then find themselves stuck in boring groups with boring people. Because these groups are not a good fit for them, they find it hard to make connections, and because it's hard to make connections, their motivation to go to socialize withers away. After a few fruitless attempts at connection, they revert back to their comfort zone and give up on making friends (until their next burst of determination, when this cycle repeats.)

Don't let that be you. Break out of the cycle of boring groups and boring people, and find the groups that give you a great chance at making friends.

The DNA of a Great Group

When you know what to look for, it's easy to identify these groups. And it's easy to know what to look for – just read on!

- **Look for groups built around something you love.**

I don't mean something that you like, or something that you kind of enjoy, but something that you love. When you have a shared passion with other members of the group, you will naturally build a quick rapport around that passion. Plus, your shared passion will give you lots to talk about, which makes building a friendship much easier.

The easiest ways to discover these kinds of groups is to do online research. A Google search for [your passion] + [your city] will often yield lots of results. Sites like meetup.com or the subReddit for your city are also great sources to look for groups related to your passion.

You're not limited to online research, either. If your passion has a shop associated with it (for instance, if your passion is sci-fi novels, then a bookstore is your shop), there's a good chance you can find like-minded folks there. Volunteering is another good option – if you love animals, volunteering at the animal shelter is a great way to give back as well as meet new people.

- ## Look for groups that your friends are involved with.

If someone you already know is in a group, they can introduce you to others and include you in conversations. It's much easier to meet new people when you have a friend to help you out.

To find out about the groups your friends are in, you have two options. The first is to just stay alert in conversation. If you ask a friend what they're doing over the weekend, and they tell you that about a group that they are attending, it's appropriate for you to express interest and ask if you could check out the group. The other option is to tell your friends that you are looking for new groups to get involved with, and ask their advice.

Both options will usually result in an invitation, although if your friends seem uncomfortable about the idea of inviting you to their groups, don't press them on it. Sometimes people like to keep their friend groups separate, so don't be offended if a friend doesn't feel comfortable with the idea of bringing you to another group.

- ## Look for groups that focus on improving people skills.

When everyone else at a group is also learning people skills, you are guaranteed to have a shared interest. Plus, these groups offer you an opportunity to learn new social skills and make new friends at the same time.

The most common of these groups is Toastmasters, which is a public speaking group. Although public speaking is different from having a conversation, practicing public speaking will greatly help your poise, confidence, and comfort in conversation.

Of course, public speaking is not the only skill that will help you in your social interactions. Partner dancing lessons are a great way to become comfortable with physical touch and to learn how to use physical contact appropriately. Improv theater classes will improve your self-confidence and teach you to think on your feet. Martial arts might improve your discipline and reduce your anxiety. You get the idea – look for groups that give you an opportunity to learn something that will improve your people skills.

- ## Look for groups that meet on a regular basis.

It's much easier to make friendships when groups meet regularly because you will have more opportunities to establish a connection with people. For instance, if the group meets weekly, then you can meet someone the first week, learn that you both enjoy fishing the second week, and then invite them to go fishing on the third week. That's much easier than having to make all of that happen the first time you meet someone, or spacing those three interactions over three months.

The Right Group for You

Remember, there's no perfect group. You might never find a group that includes all of these ideal characteristics. But your goal is not to find the perfect group – it's to find the right group for you. The principles in this lesson will help guide your search, but don't be afraid to try a group that doesn't meet all of these criteria, and don't hesitate to add your own criteria to the list.

At the end of the day, if you enjoy going to a group and you feel comfortable making friends with the people there, then it's a good group for you. Keep that in mind, and you'll have no problem finding great groups.

<u>Everyday Connections</u>

In our last lesson, we discussed how to find the right social group for you. Social groups are a great way of meeting people, and signing up for a new group is a great way to kick-start some friendships.

However, organized social groups are not your only opportunity to meet new people. Relationships can spark anytime two people interact, and great relationships can start whenever a customer chats with a waiter or travelers strike up a conversation.

Making the most of these everyday connections is easy. All you need to do is connect with others on a **person-to-person level, not a functional level.**

Here's what I mean.

Functional Interactions

When you walk into a coffee shop and order coffee from the barista, you are interacting on a functional level. You are ordering coffee, the barista is giving you coffee.

Or, perhaps you sit next to someone on a plane and only talk to them when you need to use the restroom. Again, functional level. You go to the bathroom, they get out of your way.

When you interact with people on a functional level, **you reduce them to an obstacle in your path or a means to an end**. A barista gives you a coffee fix—that's his function. A fellow traveler blocks your path to the bathroom—he's an obstacle.

But here's the thing. The barista taking your order at a coffee shop is not a robotic coffee machine; they're a person, with dreams and passions and a life outside of making cappuccinos. The person sitting next to you on the plane is not just a body blocking your path, but a fellow traveler who might be returning home from a long journey or visiting a sick loved one.

It can be hard for us to realize this, because it's easy to see the barista as a means to a coffee fix and nothing more. But when our interaction with them is completely limited to coffee, we miss our chance to connect with them on a person-to-person level.

Fortunately, it doesn't have to be that way.

Person-To-Person Connections

When you connect with someone on a person-to-person level, you lift the interaction beyond the functional level and allow real connection to take place.

To connect on a person-to-person level, just say or do something that communicate the message: "I recognize that **you are more than a means to an end.**" You can communicate this message in many different ways. You might ask a friendly personal question, or express your gratitude for the work that they're doing, or maybe just offer a warm, genuine smile.

When you acknowledge the personhood of someone else in this way, you create an opportunity for them to connect with you. Make the effort to connect on a person-to-person level, and it will be easy for others to recognize you as a person, too.

Try an experiment. Next time you go into a coffee shop, ask the person taking your order, "What do you do when you're not working?" Watch them light up when they tell you about the friends they hang out with, or the degree they're pursuing, or the kids they're raising.

And that's not limited to that one question, or to just coffee shops.

Tell the person browsing your favorite section in the bookstore that it's your favorite section, then ask them what their favorite book is.

Ask the fan standing next to you at a concert if they've ever heard the band live before.

Ask the passenger next to you on the train where they're going, or where they're coming from.

Tell the girl singing in the coffee shop that her music is beautiful, and ask what inspired her to write her songs.

Your life holds endless opportunities to connect with others. Make the extra effort to recognize the personhood of the people you encounter, and you will find yourself making connections you never thought possible.

Person-To-Person Connections

Person-to-person connections are a powerful way to connect with others, but it will take time before you become comfortable with them. Keep these simple rules in mind as you practice, and you will become an expert connector much faster.

Some People Are Not Open to Connecting.

Most people welcome the opportunity to connect on a person-to-person level, but some people will not. It's important for you to recognize when others would rather not connect, so you can respect their wishes and avoid irritating them.

For instance, if the person next to you on an airplane puts her headphones on after answering your first question, she's probably not interested in talking. If you ask the barista about his personal life, and he immediately brings the conversation back to coffee, he might prefer that you keep things professional.

Be alert to the signals that someone is not interested in connecting person-to-person and back off when you detect disinterest. A review of comfortable and uncomfortable body language will serve you well here. If someone's body language becomes uncomfortable when you start talking to them, that's a strong signal that they'd rather not talk.

Avoid Interrupting.

If you attempt to connect with someone when they are in the middle of an activity, it's possible that you'll irritate them. In general, you should feel comfortable attempting a connection if the person is already talking to you, or able to continue their current activity while chatting. But if talking to you will break their concentration on their current activity, you should be cautious about approaching them.

In other words, if you want to talk to the singer at a coffee shop, it's much better to approach when they are taking a break, rather than when they are reading their sheet music to prepare for the next song. There are exceptions, of course – that traveler in the seat next to you may be happy to put down their book and talk – but you need to be much more cautious if you plan on interrupting someone.

Start Conversations by Referencing Context.

If you turn to someone else waiting in line for a concert and the first thing you say is, "So, do you like Italian food?" you are going to come across as very weird.

But if you ask them their opinion on the band's new album, or comment on how long the line is, or ask them if they saw the band last time they were in town, the conversation will be much less awkward.

This is especially true when you want to move a conversation from functional to person-to-person. Don't suddenly go from ordering coffee to "So, what do you think about the latest Coldplay album?" It catches the barista off guard – one moment you were ordering coffee, the next you're talking about something totally different.

In order to make the transition from functional interaction to person-to-person connection feel more natural, it's best to mention the context. That's why "What do you do when you're not working?" is a perfect icebreaker question. By mentioning them working, you reference the context, and by asking them about life outside work, you open a bridge to connecting on a deeper level.

Be Prepared if Your Everyday Connection Does Not Become a Friendship.

When you connect person-to-person with someone, you will usually still go your separate ways after the conversation. You might have a great conversation with your waiter, but you are still a customer and they are still a waiter, and it is difficult to move permanently away from those roles into a friendship.

But that's ok. Even if your interaction didn't turn into a relationship, it was still a positive interaction. You learned something new about another person, and you had the chance to share something about yourself. Plus, you got the chance to practice your social skills and build your confidence.

Make Person-to-Person Connections a Part of Everyday Life.

When you make the effort to seek person-to-person connections whenever you can, you'll find that a brand new area of life has opened to you. Interactions that were previously forgettable and superficial are now meaningful. People who would have stayed strangers become friends. Person-to-person connections are your gateway to a richer life, and I encourage you to make them a part of your everyday life.

Chapter 7

Making Friends

If you followed the advice in the *Meeting People* section, you might have already made a few connections. Maybe you've checked out a few social groups or made a few everyday connections, and discovered some friendly folks.

Unfortunately, friendly folks are not the same as folks who are your friends. It's nice to feel welcomed when you attend a group meeting, but it's much more valuable to have relationships that thrive outside of the meetings.

But how do you build those relationships? It's one thing to meet someone that you get along with. It's another thing to grow your relationship with that person to the point where you feel comfortable inviting them over to hang out. Sometimes relationships will grow quickly on their own, but if they don't, how do you encourage them to grow?

Fortunately, like every other topic in this social skills guide, making friends is a skill that you can develop. With the right guidance, you'll find it easy to make lasting, fulfilling friendships. This section was written to show you how.

Making Friends contains three lessons:

- ## Finding Good Friends

  It's possible to be friends with anybody. But some people are just better friend material than others. In this section, I teach you how to identify the people who are the most likely to treat you well, and whose friendship you will most enjoy

- ## Starting a Friendship

  Once you've met someone that you want to be friends with, how do you get the relationship off the ground? In this section, I explain how to give an invitation that will open the door to a new friendship.

- ## Deepening a New Friendship

  When you've just made a new friend, it's important to nurture that friendship. This section will show you how you can grow a new friendship into a strong, lasting relationship. It also contains advice for being a good friend to others.

Finding Good Friends

When you want to make new friends, start by identifying the people who will be good friends to you.

A good friend cares about you, enjoys spending time with you, and gives you the freedom to be yourself. Good friends accept you as you are – you don't need to pretend to be someone else when you're spending time with a good friend. And although good friends might jokingly tease you, they will never bully you, disrespect you, or pressure you to do something that makes you feel uncomfortable.

You can find the people who will be good friends to you in the future by looking for the people who treat you well today. In order to do that, just ask yourself three simple questions:

"Do I Like Spending Time With This Person?"

If you don't want to spend time with someone, chances are either they won't be a good friend to you, or you won't be a good friend to them. Spending time with a friend shouldn't feel like a chore.

However, bear in mind that good friends don't need to be outwardly similar to you. It's nice to have common interests or shared experiences, but if you feel comfortable with a friend and enjoy their company, it doesn't matter if you like soccer and they like ballet. Good friendship goes beyond shared interests, so make sure that you give a fair consideration to people that might not seem similar to you at first.

"Does This Person Treat Me and Others Well?"

You will sometimes encounter people who are a lot of fun to be with, but who don't respect your opinions and beliefs, or tease you in a hurtful way, or generally just push you around. Those people are not real friends and are not worth your time.

Even if they treat you well, you might notice that they are often rude or hurtful to others. That's a warning sign that they may one day be hurtful to you. As the old saying goes, "The person who is nice to you, but rude to the waiter, or to others, is not a nice person." There are plenty of fun folks who will treat you well; don't waste your time building friendships with people who will not treat you the way a friend should.

"Does This Person Seem Like They Want to Spend Time With Me?"

Sometimes you will enjoy spending time with someone but they don't seem to have much interest in spending time with you. This is usually not a good situation to be in.

If you invest lots of time and effort trying to make friends with someone who doesn't really want to be friends with you, you will usually find yourself frustrated and worn out. It's much better to pursue friendship with someone who also wants to be friends with you.

Of course, it's possible that someone might want to spend time with you, but right now is not a good time for them. If you really want to be friends with someone, but they don't seem to want to be friends with you, it doesn't hurt to try again a few weeks or months later. But you deserve friends who are excited to spend time with you, so don't spend much time pursuing people who won't pursue you back.

Pursuing Good Friends

If you ask yourself these questions about someone and answer *no* to any of them, don't make friendship with that person a priority. That's not to say that you can't give someone a second chance – after all, first impressions are not always accurate, and it never hurts to spend some more time with someone before you rule them out.

But in general, you should focus your attention on the people who give you the best chance to be good friends. If you spend your time chasing after people who will not be good friends to you, you'll find yourself disappointed down the road.

Take a few minutes right now and use this list to think through the people you know. Find a few people who you think might be good friends to you, and keep them in mind as you read the next lesson.

Starting a Friendship

Once you know that someone is good friend material, you still need to get the friendship started.

This can be tough to do. Many people either don't know how to move the relationship from friendly acquaintance into true friendship, or they're afraid to – they don't want to offer friendship and then have it be rejected. So they wait for the other person to make the first move.

Unfortunately, if you wait for them, and they wait for you, then nothing will ever happen. You need to be willing to make the first move.

Fortunately, that first move is very simple.

All you need to do is invite the person to spend time **outside of the normal context that you see them**. If you see someone at church, invite them to come to bowling. If someone is on your bowling team, invite them to see a movie with you. You get the idea.

Choosing the Right Activity

Ideally, you should invite them to an activity that gives you the chance to talk and get to know each other. It's also good to pick an activity that the other person will enjoy. If you share a common interest or if they've told you about a particular activity they enjoy, use that to guide your invitation. If you have no idea what they're interested in, try to pick an activity that most people would enjoy (perhaps seeing a movie, or shopping in the mall).

One of my favorite invitations is to ask someone to share a meal or get some coffee together, because this means that you can focus on the conversation in a calm environment. However, it's important to pick an activity that **you** feel comfortable with. If you feel uncomfortable with the idea of an entire social encounter built around nothing but conversation, then there's no need for you to pick coffee as your activity.

And this goes beyond coffee. There might be popular social activities that you just don't enjoy, or that you don't feel comfortable doing. If the smoky atmosphere of a bar makes you feel sick, don't invite your new friend to get drinks. If large groups of people make you nervous, don't invite your partner to a concert. If you just plain hate putting, don't invite your partner to mini-golf.

This is especially good to keep in mind if you struggle with anxiety. If the thought of conversation makes you nervous, spend time with your new friend somewhere that you find relaxing and peaceful.

Of course, you should make sure that it's somewhere your partner also enjoys – but with a bit of thought, I'm sure you'll find many possible activities that both you and your partner can enjoy.

Also, one word of warning. If you invite someone of the opposite sex to hang out, they might assume that you're expressing romantic interest in them. If all you have in mind is friendship, that can be awkward, so it's best to avoid misunderstanding. (If you really are interested in dating them, that's fine – but this is the *Making Friends* chapter, and we'll cover dating later in the book)

Because of the potential for misunderstanding, you should do your best to avoid inviting friends to explicitly "date night" activities, like dinner and a movie.

It also doesn't hurt to clarify in your invitation that you are only interested in friendship. Simply saying, "Hey, I'd like to be friends," before you invite someone to hang out can help make sure everyone stays on the same page.

Your Friendship Begins

Once you choose an activity and invite someone to hang out outside of your normal context, something cool happens. Your invitation signals to them that **you want to be friends**.

Without this signal, the other person may have never even considered friendship with you. That's not because they dislike you, but simply because they never knew that you wanted to be friends with them.

But now, because you invited them to hang out outside the normal group, you show that you are interested in being friends with them. Your invitation causes them to think, "This person wants to be friends with me," and ask themselves, "Do I want to be friends with this person?"

If the two of you get along, most likely their answer will be a resounding "Yes!" to both your invitation and the resulting friendship.

Of course, they might say "No" to your invitation. But if they turn down your invitation, that doesn't necessarily mean they don't want to be friends – it could just mean they're busy or not interested in the activity you are inviting them to.

As a rule of thumb, you should **wait until someone has turned down your invitations three times** before you conclude that they don't want to hang out with you.

If you've invited them three times, you've sent a clear signal that you want to be friends. If they want to be friends back, they'll usually make the time to hang out with you.

Fortunately, most likely their answer to your invitation will not be not "No" but "Yes!" Once they reach that "Yes!" something very important happens. They stop thinking of you as "Bob, the guy from my book club" but "My friend Bob."

And once they think of you as their friend, it's no longer weird for you to call them up and ask them to hang out that weekend, or invite them to grab lunch, or see if they want to see the latest movie with you.

That's just what friends do.

Deepening a New Friendship

Ok, you've found someone who seems like quality friend material. You invited them to hang out, and they've accepted.

At this point in the relationship, you should be feeling excited. You've met a cool person, you enjoy spending time with them, and a friendship is taking off.

But you want to be careful here.

Just like a flower can wither if you give it either too much water or not enough, you want to strike a balance with how much you pursue this new friendship.

In other words, you should **pursue a new friend at a steady rate, but not one that is overwhelming**. If you hang out with a new friend once, and then start calling them every day, they're going to feel uncomfortable and may back off from the friendship.

Similarly, if you spend time with them once and never call them again, they'll probably conclude that you don't want to be friends after all.

Finding the Middle Ground

Of course, it's easy to see how either extreme causes problems, but finding the right middle ground is harder. Unfortunately, there's no perfect way to know how often to spend time with your new friend. It will depend on how well the two of you get along, and how busy your schedules are.

However, a good rule of thumb is to invite them to spend time together **at least once a month, and no more than once a week**.

Being a rule of thumb, this is obviously only a rough guideline. If you really enjoy spending time together, you may find yourself hanging out multiple times each week, and if they are very busy, you might find you can only hang out less than once per month.

If this sounds complicated, don't worry. In practice, you'll find it's simple to strike the right balance.

Just **base the frequency of your invitations to them on the frequency of their invitations to you**. If they are frequently inviting you to hang out, then you have a green light to invite them more often. If they rarely invite you to hang out, then you should probably invite them to hang out less frequently. You will quickly get a feel for what works for you and your new friend.

Becoming a Great Friend

Of course, there's more to friendship that simply knowing how often to spend time together. Growing in friendship means learning how to be a good friend.

Remember, good friends care about each other, enjoy spending time together, and give each other the freedom to be themselves. At the beginning of your friendship, you looked for someone who might be a good friend to you. Now, **be a good friend to them**.

Show that you care about your friend by asking good questions that show you want to know more about them, and by making the effort to see the world from their perspective.

Help your friend enjoy your time together by having smooth conversation, and by watching for the body language signals that tell you if they are uncomfortable.

And give your friend the freedom to be themselves by letting them know, with words and deeds, that you care about them, you believe in them, and you accept them just the way they are.

Making Friends

Making friends is an awesome, worthwhile, life changing goal. But the joy you get from having friends is only a tiny fraction of the joy you gain from being a great friend to others.

Chapter 8

Supporting Your Friends

How do you help friends who need support?

Well, there's no foolproof formula for instant success. But there are solid principles that can guide you.

They won't tell you exactly what to do because each situation is different, but they'll put you on the right track.

I've organized the principles into three categories.

First, I teach you **how to respond in the moment**. Learn the principles you need when you are face to face with a struggling friend who needs support.

Second, I teach you **how to help your friend over the long term**. Most serious problems are not solved in a single conversation, and you may need to support your friends over weeks or even months. That's why I lay out the principles that you need to support friends with long term problems.

Third, I'll teach you **how to protect yourself from burnout, manipulation, and unhealthy boundaries** when you are helping others. Lifeguards learn to protect themselves from being pulled under when rescuing a drowning swimmer, and you also need to learn how to protect yourself from harm when you are helping others.

Finally, I conclude with some encouragement.

Here's the full list of topics:

In the Moment

- Be Present

- It's Not About You

- Make Specific, Tangible Offers

- Offer Support, Not Solutions

- Don't Tell Them What to Feel

- Don't Minimize the Problem

- Don't Change the Subject

- Don't Panic

The Long Term

- Follow Up

- Don't Insist

- Educate Yourself

- Suggest Professional Help

Take Care of Yourself

- Let Your Friends Support You

- Don't Solve Their Problems for Them

- Make Sure They Want to Get Better

- Practice Self Care

Supporting Friends in the Moment

Be Present

Your job is not to give advice (although a little advice might be helpful.)

Your job is not to make them feel better (although your presence may comfort them.)

Your job is not to know the right thing to say (in fact, sometimes silence is the perfect response.)

Instead, your job is **just to be with them**. Give them a space to express their feelings. Give them a space to talk if they want. Give them the assurance that even though you can't fix their problem, they don't have to face it alone.

Henri Nouwen said it better than I ever could:

"When we honestly ask ourselves which person in our lives means the most to us, we often find that it is those who, instead of giving advice, solutions, or cures, have chosen rather to share our pain and touch our wounds with a warm and tender hand.

*The friend who can be silent with us in a moment of despair or confusion, who can stay with us in an hour of grief and bereavement, who can tolerate not knowing, not curing, not healing and face with us the reality of our powerlessness, **that is a friend who cares.**"*

It's all right to offer advice now and then. But for the most part, you should say things like, "I don't know how to fix it, but I'm here with you," or "That sounds really hard, and I'm sorry."

If you're not sure what to say, try reflecting back to them what you're hearing. For instance, you might say something like, "It sounds like the stress just keeps piling up and it feels overwhelming," or "It sounds like you're really frustrated with the way you're being treated at work."

You can also ask simple open-ended questions, such as, "So what are you going to do now?" or, "How are you holding up under all this stress?"

Remember, you're not a counselor, and it's not your job to lead your friend to new insights. Don't ask leading questions or dig into their subconscious. Instead, just do your best to give them a safe space where they can process how they're feeling.

It's Not About You

When someone shares a problem with you, it's often appropriate to share similar experiences from your own life.

For instance, if they are worried about failing a class, you might share about a time when you almost failed a class – either to empathize with them, or to encourage them that you survived and they will too.

However, there is a fine line between sharing an experience to help another person, and sharing an experience to put the spotlight on yourself.

It's okay to tell a suffering friend that you know how painful breakups can be. It's not okay to spend ten minutes complaining about your ex, or tell them, "I had that problem too and then I solved it," and talk about how great your life is now.

Be particularly careful to avoid the "bigger fish" response. The term comes from a habit among fisherman who will interrupt anyone telling a story about catching a big fish in order to tell about the time they caught an even bigger fish.

Among fishing buddies, this is a bit irritating but not a big deal. But if your friend comes to you for support, it's hurtful to respond,

"That's nothing! I'm the one who really has it rough – let me tell you about my problems..." Not only did you fail to give your friend support, but you also hurt their feelings by acting like their problem didn't matter.

You also want to avoid reacting like their problem is the biggest thing in the world (otherwise known as the "your fish is gigantic and incredibly scary" response.) Their problem might be serious, but life goes on. Don't act like their problem is the worst thing in the world, or that you have no idea how to handle it. That will just make them feel worse about the problem. No matter how you're feeling about their problem, keep your focus on them.

Bottom line: **don't make it about you.** Use stories from your own experience sparingly, and make sure to only tell stories to encourage the other person – then put the spotlight right back on them. And no matter how you feel about their problem, don't let your emotions take center stage — again, keep the spotlight on them.

Make Specific, Tangible Offers

It's good to say "I'm here for you" or "Let me know if you need anything," but it's not ideal.

Offers like this are vague – what exactly does it mean to be "here for someone?" These offers also put the onus on the other person to figure out what to ask you for, which can be a lot to ask of a suffering person.

Instead, **make specific, tangible offers**. Don't say, "Wow, that sounds rough. Let me know if I can help." Instead, say, "Wow, that sounds rough. Do you want to talk about it?"

Instead of saying, "Let me know if you need anything," ask "Would it help if I bring you a meal this week?" or "Would you like to hang out later?"

If they say no to your specific offer, it's okay to make one generic offer like, "Is there anything else I can do to help?" but start by making specific offers.

Note: when making your specific offers, be careful not to try to fix the other person's problem, and be careful not to trivialize their problem.

For instance, I remember a time I was very sad because I was mourning the death of my cat. A friend of mine noticed I was sad and said, "Let me show you cute kitten photos – that will cheer you up!" Although she meant well, her words were hurtful because they implied that my problem was trivial and could be solved with a few cat photos.

Here's some examples of good specific offers you can make:

- Do you want to talk about it?

- Do you want to get some coffee?

- Do you want to go for a walk?

- Do you want a hug?

- Want to play some video games with me?

- Can I cook a meal for you?

- Do you want advice?

- Do you want to tell me about the person you lost? [if they are in a breakup or lost a loved one]

- Can I sit next to you?

Offer Support, Not Solutions

Like most people, your immediate response to someone's problem might be trying to offer a solution.

And this is a natural response – after all, who doesn't want to solve a friend's problem?

Unfortunately, **this response usually backfires**. When a friend comes to you, they are normally looking for support, not solutions. They want to be able to talk about the issue; they want to receive encouragement and validation – they might even want a safe place to cry.

But when you immediately offer advice or try to fix the problem, you prevent your friend from finding the support they are looking for. Once they've had the opportunity to share their emotions with you, then they might be open to hearing your advice. But when they first open up to you, **they need you to listen, not to fix it.**

Honestly, your friend has probably already spent an awful lot of time thinking through their problem. While it's possible that you've thought of a solution that hasn't yet occurred to them, it's unlikely.

So be humble when offering advice.

Ask them if they want to hear your advice before you start giving it, and if they don't like your advice, drop it. They are the experts on their own problem, and if you insist on telling them what to do, you will just irritate them and make their situation worse.

Don't Tell Them What to Feel

Everyone's suffering is different.

Even if you've dealt with the exact same issue as your friend, the issue will affect you differently. So don't tell your friend empty platitudes like, "The same thing happened to me, and so I know how you must be feeling."

Instead, give them space to process their feelings. Ask gentle questions, listen attentively, and **don't rush them**.

In the moment, your friend might not really know what they're feeling. Have you ever thought you were angry, but really you were embarrassed? Or thought you were sad, but really you were lonely? Emotions are complicated. It can take time for someone to sort through their feelings and figure out what's really going on. So don't rush your friend as they work through that process.

And don't tell them, "You must be angry," or "You must be so miserable." Instead, ask questions. "Did it make you angry when she said that?" is good, although it's not great because it's a leading question. "How did you feel when she said that?" is better.

Another option is to share how YOU would feel in that situation. For instance, you might say something like "Man, if my boyfriend cheated on me, I would be furious. How are you handling it?"

By sharing your own feelings, it can help your friend process their own feelings. They might realize, "Yeah, I feel furious too," or "Actually, I don't feel furious – I feel relieved. I guess I'm glad the relationship is over."

Most importantly, you should never tell them to "get over it" or "pull yourself together." As with a physical wound, emotional wounds take time to heal. An injured person can't make a broken bone heal faster through willpower, and a suffering person can't heal emotionally faster through willpower.

It takes time – don't rush them.

Don't Minimize the Problem

When a friend brings a serious problem to you, it may be tempting to minimize the problem so you don't have to deal with it.

Your first impulse may be to say, "Oh, it's not that bad," or "Don't get so emotional about it," or even "This isn't that big of a deal."

However, this is usually the last thing that a struggling friend wants to hear. Even if it's objectively not a big deal, it FEELS like a big deal to them (or else they wouldn't have asked you for support.) Meet them where they're at. **If it feels like a big deal to them, treat it like a big deal.**

You also need to avoid the temptation to minimize their problem by blaming them for it ("I'm sorry you're stressed about your bad grade, but it's your fault for not studying.")

Sometimes people do cause their own problems, but even if the problem is 100% their fault, it doesn't help for you to point that out. Your job is to be a supportive friend, not to assign blame.

So give them space to express their feelings. Help them explore why this feels like such a big deal to them. You may want to gently provide perspective – perhaps reminding them that even with this problem, there are still a lot of good things in their life, or encouraging them to see that the current problem is temporary.

But don't tell them what they're feeling is wrong, or that they just need to "get over it." Accept that their problem is a big problem to them, and support them without trying to correct them.

Don't Change the Subject

Do you get uncomfortable when someone brings up a serious problem?

It's very difficult to respond when someone tells you that the cancer came back, or their parents are getting divorced, or they are failing their classes. A common response is to shift to a more lighthearted topic – usually after a brief, awkward pause.

But what if the person really needed to talk about their problem? What if they took a big leap of courage to tell you how they were really doing – and then you changed the topic as if nothing had happened?

Most of the time when someone brings up a problem with you, it's because they want to talk about it. It's deeply comforting to have someone care enough to listen to your problems, so you can help your friend just by listening.

I know it's uncomfortable to listen to a problem when you can't fix it, but trust me. **You make a difference just by listening.**

So as a rule of thumb – if someone wants to talk about a problem they're having, make yourself available to listen. Ask them questions. **Be curious and supportive**. Don't try to fix it, but let them know that you are on their side.

If they want to change the topic, let them. But if they're not afraid to talk about their pain, you should be brave, too.

Don't Panic

Let's say you get sick, so you decide to visit the doctor.

As you explain your symptoms, the doctor looks more and more concerned, until she finally starts flailing her arms, running around the room and screaming "OH NO YOU HAVE PNEUMONIA I'M FREAKING OUT RIGHT NOW AAH!"

It's a ridiculous image – because we expect that, no matter what's wrong with us, the doctor is going to calmly help us get better.

And when your friend comes to you with a problem, they also expect you to **be calm and help them get better.** I'm not saying that you need to be an unemotional robot – it's fine to get emotional, or even to cry with your friend.

But remember that your job is to support your friend, and sometimes that means that you need to put your own emotions to the side so you can be a good helper. There will be time later for you to process your feelings – but if you freak out when your friend needs you, then you can't support them.

Again, **your friend is the one having the problem, not you**. If you are ever more emotional than your suffering friend, that's a good sign that you should calm down and refocus on helping them.

We've finished Part 1: In the Moment. Our next pages are from Part 2: The Long Term.

Supporting a Friend Long Term

Follow Up

Big problems don't go away overnight.

If you learn a friend is struggling with a significant problem, they'll probably still be struggling down the road. **Help them out by remembering to check in.**

For instance, if your friend shares a struggle they're having, it might be appropriate to text them the next day to say "Hey, I'm thinking of you and I'm behind you 100%" or call them a few days later to invite them to coffee.

If you know a friend is having a hard time in general (maybe they are struggling with depression or recovering from a breakup), be deliberate to occasionally ask them how they are doing – and stick around to hear the real answer. People will often withdraw from social interaction when they are depressed, so **reach out to them if you haven't seen them for a while**.

Remember, your friend might be in so much pain that they don't want to talk about their problem. I know that when I am going through a breakup, the last thing I want to do is talk about it – the pain is still too raw.

If they don't want to talk about it, provide them with some positive interactions that aren't focused around their problem. Invite them to hang out with you at the mall, or see a movie together, or go for a run. Basically, invite them to remember the good parts of life, and give them a respite from brooding over their loss.

It's possible they won't want to do any of these things – sometimes when you are suffering, you can't enjoy normal activities. But **even if they say no, it helps to know that you cared enough to ask**.

It makes a huge difference to have a friend care enough to check in. Don't let your friend drop off the radar. If you know they're struggling, follow up on a regular basis and make sure they know you care about them. Invite them to coffee. Let them know you care. Give them a call.

They'll be glad you did.

Don't Insist

Sometimes, the best thing you can do is back off.

Maybe the other person doesn't really want to talk about their problem, or they don't feel close enough to you to open up – or maybe they're already getting great support from someone else.

If you insist on helping, **you can easily make their situation worse**. Now they have to deal with their problem AND an annoying wannabe helper.

If you're a guy, you want to be especially careful here. It's common for guys to convince themselves that girls need their help (especially when they're attracted to her), and insisting that a girl accept your help is a sure way to annoy her. If she needs your help, she'll ask you for it. If you cared about her, you would respect her *no* instead of looking for an opportunity to show off.

But whatever the gender of the person you're helping — offer your support, and then if they choose not to take it, let it go.

I usually try to ask twice – for instance, "It looks like you're feeling down. Do you want to talk about it?"

If they say no, I might add, "Are you sure? I'm here for you if you need me." If they turn me down again, then I let it go and change the topic.

Even if they do choose to talk about it, **don't assume they want you to solve their problem.** Several months ago, I had a friend who complained to me about a problem she was having. I suggested she do something to solve her problem, and when she decided she didn't like my idea, I went ahead and did it for her.

At the time, I thought I was being helpful. But when I told her what I had done, she was very upset. She explained that she was responsible for solving the problem, not me, and because I had done it for her, it communicated that I didn't trust her to take care of herself. Needless to say, this caused her to feel very hurt and disrespected.

Don't make the same mistake as me – if you offer someone a solution and they don't take it, don't insist on it.

If you offer support and they turn you down, let it go. Let the suffering person be in charge.

Educate Yourself

It's hard to help when you don't understand what they're dealing with. So do some homework on your friend's struggles.

If they have a diagnosed mental health condition (like depression or anorexia), find a book or some reputable websites that talk about those conditions.

Another option is organizations that provide support. To Write Love On Her Arms (twloha.com) is a great organization that provides advice and encouragement for many common struggles.

Of course, your friend can also educate you – they are the expert on their own struggle. They might not want to talk about their struggle, but usually people are happy to open up about how their problems affect them.

If you do talk to your friend about their struggles, **remember to suspend judgment**. It might not make sense to you why a breakup is so painful or why depression makes it so hard to get out of the bed in the morning. But your friend has no reason to lie to you, so if they're telling you something about their situation, it's probably accurate.

Again, **your friend is the expert on their own struggle**. Don't disagree with them about their experiences, or invalidate their feelings.

Instead, be a curious student. Ask questions and let them know you want to learn everything you can in order to help them better. **The more you know, the more you can help.**

Suggest Professional Help

You wouldn't try to set a friend's broken leg just because you've watched some Grey's Anatomy.

Similarly, a few self-help books or a psychology class do not make you a therapist. So don't act like one! If you think your friend needs professional help, please refer them to a counselor.

It might be a good idea for your friend to see a counselor if:

- They are very unhappy.
- They can't enjoy normal things in life.
- Their performance in work or school is suffering.
- They're using substances (like drugs or alcohol) to cope with the problem.
- They are in an unhealthy or abusive relationship.
- The problem has persisted for a long time and hasn't gotten better.

Of course, if you have any problems that fit these descriptions, please see a counselor too!

Most importantly: if your friend is talking about hurting themselves or someone else, or if they match any of the other warning signs of suicide, then it is very important that you get them to see a counselor as soon as possible. **If you ever think they may be in immediate danger of suicide, you should call 911** (or whatever your local emergency number is.)

Although counselors can seem expensive, most health insurance covers counseling, and many colleges have counseling centers that are free to students. In addition, some counselors offer "sliding scale" fees where people with lower incomes pay lower rates. **Money should never be an obstacle to getting counseling.**

Not sure how to find a therapist? PsychologyToday.com and GoodTherapy.org have lists of therapists that you can look through to find a good match. You can also find online therapist at Breakthrough.com (although this is not available in all areas.)

Many therapists will do a free phone consultation, so a good strategy is to research a few therapists that seem good, give each of them a call, and then book a session with the one that seems like the best fit.

If you start seeing a therapist and they don't actually end up being a good fit, that's okay – just find someone else! You'll know it's a good idea to look for a new therapist if you really don't get along with your therapist at all in the first session, or if you don't see any progress by the fourth session.

There's no such thing as a perfect therapist, but **most therapists are pretty good**. So if you or your friend is really struggling, reach out to a therapist today.

That's all for Part 2: The Long Term. Next up is Part 3: Take Care of Yourself

Taking Care of Yourself

Let Your Friends Support You

In a healthy friendship, **both people give, and both people receive**.

At times one person might be doing most of the giving or receiving, but over time, it should average out.

Or to put it another way: In a normal healthy friendship, sometimes you support your friend, and sometimes your friend supports you. If you are always supporting your friend and they never support you (or vice versa), that should raise a red flag.

Now, sometimes doing 100% of the giving is the right thing to do – for instance, maybe your friend is in a crisis and they can't give back yet.

But usually, if you are doing all of the giving, then it signifies a problem. This is especially true if the one-sided giving lasts for a long period of time.

In that case, I would step back and take stock of the relationship. Is it possible that the other person is taking advantage of you?

It's likely you are being taken advantage of if you feel like the other person guilts you into giving, or if the other person never does any work to improve their own situation.

It's also possible that you might be more comfortable in the giving role, and you are resistant to receiving. This is especially likely if you are in the giving role in almost all of your close relationships.

You might wonder why someone would feel more comfortable in the giving role (after all, it's more work.) Simple: **when you are the giver, you are the one with the power.** You don't have to be dependent or vulnerable; instead, the other person is dependent on you.

I used to be like that.

Early in life, I thought, "I don't know if people will want me, but if I can make them need me, then they will stick around." So I worked to make myself indispensable to others. I offered support, encouragement, advice – and I never asked for anything in return.

The problem? The resulting relationships were shallow and unfulfilling.

I knew a lot about the other person, but they didn't know much about me. They could always call me when they needed a friend, but when I was having a hard time I suffered through it alone.

Eventually, I realized that I was being foolish, and I started opening up to my friends.

I started showing them the real me, started sharing my struggles, my dreams, my quirks. And you know what? They accepted me just as I was. **I didn't need to be needed to be wanted.**

And neither do you. So if you find that your relationships are mostly one-way, start sharing the real you with your friends. I think you'll be glad you did.

Don't Solve Others' Problems for Them

It's tempting to step in and solve your friends' problems for them.

But if you do something that your friend should do themselves, then it creates dependency and makes it easy for them to take advantage of you.

During my college years, a classmate didn't do his part of a group project. Instead of telling the teacher, I just did his work for him.

As you might guess, during the next project his work was once again incomplete, and I once again felt the need to step in and do his job as well as my own. Once I confronted him and told him that I would no longer cover for him, his work magically improved.

Of course, there is a balance here. Sometimes taking some responsibilities off a friend's plate can provide them with a big boost.

A few years ago, I was moving and felt very stressed about getting everything done. My roommate took the initiative to disassemble my desk and prepare it for moving (a major project that would have taken me a lot of time.) His help really reduced my stress levels and made me feel cared for and supported.

So I'm not saying that you should never do something that your friend can do for themselves. Instead, I'm warning you to look for patterns.

If you start to feel obligated to do something for your friend that they should normally do for themselves, or if they expect you to do things for them while they laze about, that's a sign that you probably need to rethink how you support that friend. If you're not sure, **try saying, "No," sometimes and see what happens.**

In addition, be careful to maintain good emotional boundaries. You need to be able to live your life even if your friend is struggling. If you can't feel happy as long as your friend is struggling, or if you feel personally responsible for your friend's recovery, **it's likely your boundaries have collapsed.**

Remember, **you are not responsible for your friend. Your friend is responsible for themselves**.

Decide what is appropriate for you to give, and trust your friend to do the rest.

Make Sure Your Friend Wants to Get Better

I had a friend in college who would frequently message me right before I was going to go to bed and share a problem that she wanted to talk about. I stayed up late talking with this girl numerous times, sacrificing my sleep (and sometimes, my grades!) to give her encouragement and support.

However, my friend:

- Would never see a counselor, despite my requests.

- Would always wait until late at night to bring her problems to me – she would never discuss them during the day even when I gave her the opportunity.

- Would never do anything to improve her situation. (For instance, she would spend hours and hours complaining to me about her boyfriend, but she refused to break up with him or ask him to improve his behavior.)

Ultimately, I realized that she didn't really want to get better – part of her that wanted the "victim" identity, and she liked the power that her pain gave her over other people. For instance, I think she may have waited until late at night to talk to me because she felt important when I sacrificed my sleep for her.

She wasn't faking it, exactly – a lot of bad things happened to her, and she was genuinely unhappy. But she did not want to get better, and I couldn't force her to get better against her will.

Ultimately the sacrifices I made to support and encourage her were wasted. All of my efforts only served to pull me down, not to bring her up.

So what does this mean for you? Basically – be careful when it seems like the other person is not an active participant in their recovery. If they expect you to sacrifice for them but they won't do basic things to improve their own situation, **something is wrong and you need to protect yourself.**

You don't need to cut ties or do anything drastic, but if there is strong evidence they don't want to get better, then it might be reasonable for you to require them to invest in their recovery before you will make more sacrifices for them.

For instance, I should have told her, "I know you are feeling bad tonight, but I think what you really need right now is to talk to a counselor, not to talk to me. Once you schedule an appointment with a counselor, I'll be happy to talk with you about your problems again."

Of course, it can sometimes be hard to tell if someone is trying to get better, because sometimes things that seem really easy (like scheduling an appointment with a counselor) can be really hard for someone who is struggling with depression or another mental health issue. Don't give up on a friend just because they're not doing everything you think they should be doing. It's always better to err on the side of generosity.

But if over time you see a pattern of the person not working to get better, then it may be time to put some boundaries in place. Not only will this protect you from burnout, but it may also show the other person that they are caught in a self-destructive pattern.

Practice Self Care

If you go too long without sleeping or eating, you'll collapse.

It doesn't matter how strong you are – your body has physical limits, and when you reach them you will shut down.

Similarly, if you go too long without taking care of yourself emotionally, you will burn out or melt down. It doesn't matter if you are Mr. Rogers or Mother Teresa – even the most loving people in the world can't take care of others unless they take care of themselves, too.

The bottom line: **If you want to take care of other people, you need to take care of yourself.**

Therapists call this idea "self-care" but you can call it whatever you want. Just make sure you do it!

To help you figure out if you need better self-care, I've written up some questions you should ask yourself. Take some time to think through these questions now.

Physical

- Are you getting enough sleep?

- Are you eating three meals a day?

- Are you able to exercise?

Relational

- Do you have people you talk to about your problems?

- Do you spend time with people just to have fun, not so you can support them?

- Are you able to say "No" to your friends when you need to?

Balance

- Do you have time to do the things you enjoy (hobbies, etc.?)

- Can you be happy even when you know your friend is still struggling?

- Are you able to take care of your personal responsibilities? (Schoolwork, your job, etc.?)

- Are you able to pursue personal goals and dreams that are important to you?

If you answer "No" to any of these questions, it may be a sign that you should prioritize self-care.

If you answer "No" to a lot of these questions, you need to take better care of yourself or you will burn out. (You may also want to talk to a counselor about setting better boundaries.)

Remember, nobody needs you to be a superhero. It's wonderful that you are supporting your friend, and sometimes it can feel like you need to burn yourself out to be a true friend.

But you can't help anyone if you burn out — and **if you don't take care of yourself, you will burn out**. Remember that your life matters too, and your friend wants you to be happy even if they are not.

Chapter 9

Dating

Dating is a big deal.

Romantic comedies and love songs tell us that all our problems will be solved if we just find the one right person. Online dating is a multi-billion dollar industry. And everything from prom dances to Valentine's Day seems to exist to extol the virtues of dating.

And the truth is, dating can be wonderful. Having a special someone to share your experiences with makes life sweeter and having someone who knows you deeply can help you understand yourself better too.

But dating can also be very destructive.

It's easy to develop an unhealthy dependency on the person you are dating, or for manipulation and disrespect to poison the affection that you share.

Fortunately, a little knowledge goes a long way in avoiding these problems. There are bedrock principles that will help you make sure your dating relationships are healthy, positive, and life-giving for both you and your partner.

Since I value lasting, intimate relationships, I discuss more than just how to get a girl or guy's attention. This section will guide you all the way from your first meeting to a long-term relationship, and will show you the pitfalls to avoid along the way.

And since this is a social skills guide after all, I'll also address the social skills of dating. How to ask someone out, what to do on that first date – I'll cover it all. Here's what we'll cover:

- ### Healthy Relationships Defined

  What is a healthy relationship, and why is it important?

- ### How to Have a Healthy Relationship

  How do you make sure that your relationship is healthy, positive and fulfilling?

- ### Beginning a Romance

  How do you start a romance on the right foot? Where do you go to meet your next partner?

- ### From Friendship to First Kiss

  How do you move from friendship to romance? How do you let someone know you like them?

- ### Building a Relationship Worth Having

  Once you've started a relationship, how do you get closer to your partner? How do you make your relationship stays healthy?

- ### Slow and Steady Wins Their Heart

  How do time and commitment play into your relationship?

- ### Slow and Steady Wins Their Heart, Part 2

  How do you grow in physical and emotional intimacy, without damaging the relationship?

Healthy Relationships Defined

Ok. Let's get philosophical for a second.

I know you probably want to jump ahead to the more "practical" portion of this section. You want to know how to ask someone out, what to do on a date – and trust me, we'll get there.

But those skills are useless if you don't know how to have a healthy relationship. In fact, they can be worse than useless, because being in an unhealthy relationship is often much worse than being single.

So let's take the time to go over some foundational principles of healthy relationships (because remember, the foundation is everything.)

But before I start, one important note.

There's a big difference between a relationship that is unhealthy and a relationship that is abusive. Good-hearted, well-intentioned people can easily slip into relationships that are unhealthy, and although sometimes the right response to an unhealthy relationship is to end it, often a little work can make those relationships healthy again.

In contrast, if you are in an abusive relationship, **you need to get out and you need to get help**. And if someone you know might be in an abusive relationship, you need to tell someone and get help for them.

Take a minute and Google for "warning signs of abusive relationship" right now. Seriously, I'll wait.

Even if you will never be in an abusive relationship, knowing the signs will help you recognize when a friend is at risk of being abused. And if you recognize those signs in your relationship or a friend's relationship, you should call a domestic abuse hotline and tell someone what's going on.

Healthy Relationships: A Love Story

Still with me? Cool.

Let's move on to how to make sure your relationship is healthy. But what do I mean by a healthy relationship?

Well, let me tell you a story.

My senior year of college, I dated a girl named Sam, who is a wonderful young woman with a loving soul and an incredible gift for art.

One evening, Sam asked me "Daniel, what is your goal for our relationship?"

I replied, "Sam, I want the people who know you and love you the best to be able to say '**We are so glad that Daniel dated Sam**, because he made her really happy, and because he helped her become more the person that she was supposed to be.'"

My relationship with Sam is now over, but I still take a great deal of joy in the knowledge that I did my best to live out that answer. I accepted Sam for who she was, brought joy to her life, and encouraged her to grow more into the person she was supposed to be.

And you know what? Sam accepted me for who I was, brought joy to my life, and encouraged me to grow more into the person I was supposed to be.

That is a healthy relationship in a nutshell. It was a relationship in which we accepted and cherished each other, where we encouraged each other to grow, and where we were more focused on giving to each other than receiving from each other.

It was also a healthy relationship because of what we did not do. We didn't disrespect or manipulate each other. We didn't drop everything else in our life to focus solely on each other. We didn't pressure each other to change (we encouraged each other to grow, but we always accepted each other for who we were, not for who we might be in the future.) And we didn't rush things – we let the relationship grow at a natural, healthy pace.

Committing to Healthy Relationships

My relationship with Sam was a wonderful part of my life, and I want you to have wonderful, healthy relationships too.

But I'll be honest. Healthy dating relationships take work. They require that you dedicate yourself to your partner's well-being and happiness, and that you swallow your pride and your selfishness. They require a willingness to make short-term sacrifices so that you can have lasting joy.

They require a commitment, in short. And commitments are hard.

But when you have experienced the joy of a truly healthy relationship, **you won't ever want to settle for anything less.** I hope that when you enter your next relationship, you commit to making it a healthy one – both for your sake, and the sake of your partner.

Of course, even if you are fully committed to a healthy relationship, wanting a healthy relationship is not the same as knowing how to get there. Fortunately, the next lesson explains in detail "How to Have a Healthy Relationship" and contains all of the practical information you need to know.

How to Have a Healthy Relationship

If you've read the previous lesson, you hopefully understand why healthy relationships are important.

Now, it's time to learn the details of what makes a relationship healthy (or unhealthy.)

Because every relationship is different, there's no way to make an exhaustive list of all the ways relationships could be healthy or unhealthy. But if you focus on the most important things, you will avoid the vast majority of problems.

With that in mind, I've listed the three major principles that need to be true for any relationship to be healthy. Learn these three principles, and you'll know how to have a healthy, fulfilling romance.

Ready? Let's dive in.

Freedom and Acceptance

In a healthy relationship, both partners feel accepted, and have the freedom to be themselves.

That means that both partners should be able to relax and be themselves, without worrying that the other partner will judge them for their thoughts or actions. **You should never need to hide part of yourself to be accepted by your partner.**

Of course, this doesn't mean that your partner has to approve of everything that you do. If you're making a bad decision, I hope your partner speaks up to let you know!

But you shouldn't feel that you have to agree with their opinions for them to accept you, and you shouldn't feel like you need your partner's permission to make your own decisions about your life.

Even when you disagree, you should still respect each other's opinions. If your partner belittles your opinions and beliefs, or doesn't treat you like an equal, that's a serious sign of an unhealthy relationship.

In addition, you should both feel that you have the freedom to talk about the relationship, and to bring up problems that you see. If my partner does something that upsets me, I should be able to (gently) let her know.

And if she sees a problem in our relationship, she should be able to let me know so we can find a solution. **Both partners are equal members of the relationship**, so they should have equal say about what happens in the relationship.

Meaningful Lives Outside the Relationship

In a healthy relationship, both partners have fulfilling lives outside of their dating relationship and maintain close friendships with people other than their dating partner. In addition, both partners support each other to pursue those important parts of life that are outside of the dating relationship.

It's not uncommon for people to let everything else in their life slide when they start a new relationship. They stop spending time with friends or pursuing their goals because the new relationship quickly takes up all of their time.

This is unhealthy.

A dating relationship should be a significant part of your life, but it's only **part** of your life.

You should still have other close relationships, as well as hobbies that you enjoy and life goals that you pursue. Your relationship shouldn't be the only thing you spend your free time on, nor should it be the only important thing in your life.

In addition, your partner should support you in your outside relationships, hobbies, and goals. Your partner should encourage you to get that degree, or to sign up for that bowling league, or to spend some time with that friend that you haven't seen in a while.

And you should encourage your partner in the same way – even if that means they spent less time with you. If it's important to them, it should be important to you.

Shared Selflessness

In a healthy relationship, both partners make it their goal for their partner to be happy and fulfilled, not to have their partner make them happy and fulfilled.

This is the most important point. So listen carefully, and please make sure you understand what I'm saying.

If you are more concerned with what your partner can do for you than with what you can do for your partner, then you should not be dating them.

And if they are more concerned with what you can do for them than with what they can do for you, then they should not be dating you.

It's natural to think about the good things our partner can do for us – they give us someone to talk to, alleviate our loneliness, and feel really nice to kiss or hold. And it's ok to want those things, and to enjoy them.

But your goal in your relationship should not be to get everything you can from your partner. It should be to give everything you can to your partner, because after all, **giving is what love is all about.**

Of course, your partner should also have this motive.

If you give everything you can to your partner, but your partner rarely gives to you, then they are taking advantage of you (and you shouldn't be dating them.) Stay away from the trap of "If only I gave more/became a better partner, maybe my partner would start to give to me."

The Beauty of Interdependence

But hopefully, you do care about your partner, and they do care about you. And when that is true, something incredible happens.

You can stop worrying so much about yourself, and instead focus on meeting their needs. And they can stop worrying so much about themselves, and instead focus on meeting your needs. You trust your partner to take care of you, and they trust you to take care of them.

There is a beautiful interdependence that is created, where the two of you can rest in each other's presence and know that you are safe and loved and accepted. You can trust that you don't have to have it all together, because your partner has your back, and loves you even when you make mistakes.

One day, you might be presented with the opportunity to settle for a relationship that is unhealthy and superficial. Don't do it.

The beauty and joy of a healthy, interdependent relationship is an experience like none other, and it's worth the wait. Don't cheat yourself by settling for something less.

Of course, you can't get to that point of interdependence without first starting the relationship.

Beginning a Romance

Ok. You've read through the explanation of a healthy relationship, and you're excited to experience a great relationship with that special someone.

So... now what?

With a few exceptions, your perfect partner is not going to drop from the sky into your waiting arms. You need to meet them first, and then get to know them, and then take the plunge of admitting your feelings and entering the strange and wonderful world of more-than-friends.

But with a little guidance, that process can be exciting and joyful, instead of confusing and scary. Let's walk through each of the steps in turn.

Meeting Your Partner

Forget singles events and awkwardly trying to pick up people at bars.

You should meet potential romantic partners in the exact same way that you would meet new friends. This flies against a lot of conventional wisdom, I know.

But hear me out – there is an important reason why I believe this is true.

When you go to an event for the express purpose of meeting a romantic partner, **you're much more likely to link up with someone who is a bad fit for you**. Because the pressure is on, you are probably going to focus on making a good impression, instead of putting your focus on getting to know the people you meet.

Authenticity and vulnerability (the building blocks of real connection and intimacy) go out the window, and superficial attractiveness and charm take the spotlight.

The result? You zero in on the folks who are the most superficially attractive – not the people who will be the best long-term partner for you.

The solution? Take the time to get to know that attractive guy/girl as a person before you start thinking about them as a potential romantic partner.

True Attraction

It's fine to be initially attracted to someone. But take a step back and remind yourself that you don't really know them yet. Just like there is true fear and physical fear, there is true attraction and physical attraction.

You want to wait for true attraction – which is the sweet moment where you realize you **like the other person for who they are, not for what they can offer you**. And that true attraction takes time to build.

And when I say it "takes time to build," I'm referring to days or weeks, not minutes. I know that seems dull and unromantic (what happened to love at first sight?) But remember that the foundation is everything, and it takes time to make a good foundation for your relationship.

If you take the time to really get to know the other person, you will build your romance on a rock-solid foundation of true attraction. Rush in, and your relationship will balance precariously on the shaky foundation of physical attraction.

Application

Here's how you put this in action.

First, check your motives. Finding a dating partner should not be your primary motive for meeting new people. It's fine to have that be part of your motives, but it shouldn't be your number one.

The primary motive of "find a date" means that you're missing out on the chance to make good friendships with people that don't ping your "possible date" radar. Plus (like I explain above), when your primary motive is finding a date, it's actually much harder for you to find a good dating partner.

So take the time to think through your motives. If you find that your primary motive is in fact finding a dating partner, don't despair. Just spend some time speaking truth to yourself, and remind yourself of the reasons for getting to know people as people, instead of as potential dates.

Second, shake up your routine. If you're not going to dating-focused events, you need another way to meet people. If you keep going to the same events or spending time with the same groups, your opportunities to meet new people will be very limited.

So try new things. Sign up for a class in a topic that interests you. Join a volunteer group. Make a rule that you'll try one new thing every week, or make a list of new groups to check out.

Of course, this advice will also help you with life in general. Shaking up your routine is a surefire way to make new friends, enrich your life, and discover new passions. But it's also extremely applicable to finding a dating partner – every new thing you try is another opportunity to meet that special someone.

Third, pursue deep connections. Remember when I said you want to get to know that attractive guy/girl as a person before you start dreaming about them as your boyfriend/girlfriend? Well, that requires that you make a point of getting to know people.

So pursue deep connections with people. Try to push past superficial conversations about the weather or the latest movie and try to learn the story of the people you are talking with. Find out what makes them unique; ask them about their passions and their dreams – and share your story with them in response.

Of course, making deep connections takes time, and it takes practice. Some people won't be open to connecting, and that's fine. You should always be ready to steer the conversation away from personal topics if you sense the other person becoming uncomfortable, and it's often wise to take gradual steps towards a deep connection when you're not sure if the other person will be comfortable.

But give people the opportunity to connect – don't assume they will say no. Ask questions that show your genuine interest in the other person. Share parts of your own story to let the other person know that sharing is ok.

If the other person sees that you genuinely want to get to know them, they almost always will respond positively to your attempts to connect. Most people really want to connect with others – they just want someone else to make the first move.

So make a point of connecting with everyone you can. I think if you do, you'll find your life blessed with new friends, good conversations, and perhaps (one day soon) a new special someone.

Moving Beyond Friendship

Ok. Let's say you resisted short-sighted "find a date at all costs" motives, you shook up your routine, and you're making a genuine effort to connect with the new people you've met.

And let's say that one of those new people has connected with you in a special way, and after getting to know him/her as a person, you're ready to enter the strange and beautiful world of more-than-friends.

Now what? Well, now we move from friendship to first kiss. Let's go.

From Friendship to First Kiss

Ok. Let's say you've spent the time to get to know this new person. You enjoy spending time with them, you feel close to them, and they seem to enjoy spending time with you too.

Plus, you've sorted through your emotions and you feel that true attraction is starting to build – this is more than a crush. And you've taken a look at how the two of you interact to make sure you don't see any warning signs of an unhealthy relationship.

You're ready to move the relationship into dating territory, in other words.

But how do you do it?

Well, there's no one right way. Relationships are different because people are different, so your love story will be different than the couple down the road.

But in general, there's three simple steps that you can follow.

First, **gauge their interest.**

Second, **signal your interest.**

Third, **declare your interest.**

Ready? Let's tackle each in turn.

Gauge Their Interest

This one can be tough.

People will often treat a good friend and a romantic interest in a very similar way, so it's easy to get a false positive.

It IS possible to tell when someone is romantically interested in you, but it's hard, and it requires a lot of practice. You need to experience several people interacting with you as a friend and also several people interacting with you as a romantic interest before you can reliably tell the difference between the two.

Because of this, the best way to tell if someone is interested in you is to **compare the way they interact with you with the way they interact with others of your gender.**

If someone is very physically affectionate with you, but they're also very physically affectionate with their other close friends, that's not a signal that they're interested in you. If someone spends lots of time with you one-on-one, and they rarely hang out with other friends one-on-one, that's a much more positive signal.

Signal Your Interest

If you have a reasonable suspicion the person is interested in you, it's time to let them know that you are interested too.

However, you shouldn't force them into a decision. At this stage, you want to give them the chance to get used to the thought of dating you, without the pressure of a commitment.

In other words, ask them on a date, but don't ask them to be your boyfriend/girlfriend.

Now, if you followed the advice in the guide, you've already spent some time with this person and gotten to know them. So if you ask them to spend some more time together, you're not sending a clear signal of interest.

Instead, invite them to something that feels like a traditional date – dinner and a movie, a school dance, etc.

Put some effort into making it feel romantic, and feel free to be more flirty, but don't go overboard. You want to be the same person they

144

got to know pre-dating, so if you act artificially romantic, it will make them uncomfortable.

Mostly, just relax and enjoy the evening. Your date is an opportunity to get a hint of what a relationship would be like, so the goal is not to woo your partner but to give the two of you a chance to consider the idea of more-than-friends.

They might ask if it's a date, in which case you should be honest and say yes. The point is not to be coy about your interest but rather to share your interest in a way that doesn't force them to immediately decide if they are interested in you.

Declare Your Interest

After you go on a date (or two) and all goes well, it's time to share the way you feel.

This doesn't have to be an elaborate affair. Just pick a time when you're both relaxed, find a quiet place, and speak from the heart. Don't worry about flowery language or being romantic – just be honest.

It's ok to share your feelings in a creative way. For instance, if the thought of sharing your feelings out loud terrifies you, perhaps you could write them a letter (of course, make sure you're there when they read it!)

When you've shared how you feel, give them some space to share how they feel. It's possible that they're not sure yet, or they need more time to get to know you. So be willing to talk through their feelings with them, and be willing to wait for an answer if they're not ready yet.

A Brief Note on Rejection

It's also possible that they don't share your feelings.

Usually you would have found this out before you explicitly shared your feelings, but sometimes you have to put all your cards on the table before you learn how someone really feels.

If that's the case, it's going to suck. It's hard to tell someone you like them, and find that they don't like you back (at least, not romantically.) So you're going to have to deal with some pain, and it's important to acknowledge that pain and not bottle it up or ignore it.

But **it will be ok**.

You don't need to date someone to be happy. And although you felt a special connection with this person, you will find that special connection with someone else in the future.

And in the meantime, you can have a wonderful friendship with this person that you've grown fond of. Instead of being angry that you can't have a romance with that person, be grateful for the friendship that you can enjoy.

It will take some work to retrain your heart, but it can be done.

(Of course, this advice applies more to relationships that never really get off the ground rather than to breakups of committed relationships. Once you and your partner have become boyfriend and girlfriend with someone, it is much harder—although still possible—to return to a state of close friendship. But we'll discuss breakups later)

More-Than-Friends

I needed to address rejection because it can happen, and you need to be prepared for it.

But although you need to prepare for it, it's probably not likely. If they don't share your feelings, you probably would have figured that out when attempting to gauge their interest, or they would have let you know when you invited them on that first date.

So most likely, when you take the plunge and admit your affection, you will find that your partner returns that affection.

In that case, congratulations! The start of a relationship is an incredible experience, and a special, wonderful time of your life is just beginning.

Building a Relationship Worth Having

Ok. You've found that special someone, expressed your interest, and got the "Yes!"

Now, it's time to enjoy the wonderful process of getting to know your new partner and growing deeper in intimacy, affection, and love.

However, there's a right way and a wrong way of doing this.

The wrong way (that many couples fall into), is to rush into the relationship full throttle. You may have been cautious when gauging the other person's interest, but now that the relationship is official, any thought of brakes go out the window.

You share your deepest, darkest secrets with them. You let yourself get so emotionally attached that a breakup would devastate you. And you remove all limits from your physical affection – all before the relationship is two weeks old!

The Dangers of Full Throttle Intimacy

There's a reason I call this the "wrong way" of going about relationships. Your relationship needs time to grow if you want it to be healthy.

Think back to your last Thanksgiving dinner.

The turkey has to stay in the oven for hours before it's ready, and there's no way to shortcut the process.

If you crank the oven temperature up to 1000 degrees, you're not going to get a delicious turkey in five minutes – you're going to light the turkey on fire (and possibly burn your house down.)

This same principle works in relationships.

It takes time for true intimacy to build.

It takes time for someone to truly earn your trust.

It takes time for two people to learn to love each other well.

And if you're not willing to give it that time, you run the risk of having a relationship that ends up like our scorched Thanksgiving turkey. You don't want that – and what's more, you don't want to inflict that on your partner.

The "Slow and Steady" Square

Of course, you don't want to go too fast – but you also don't want to stand still. So how do you know that your relationship is growing at a healthy pace?

A very handy rule of thumb is something I call the "Slow and Steady" Square

In a square, there are four equal sides. If every side increases by the same amount, then each side is still equal and you still have a square.

If some sides increase but others do not, then you no longer have a square.

For the "Slow and Steady" Square, think of the four sides of the square as Time, Commitment, Physical Intimacy, and Emotional Intimacy. You want each of those four sides to go up at more-or-less the same rate, so that you keep a square.

In other words, as you spend time with your partner, you want commitment, physical intimacy, and emotional intimacy to increase at similar rates. And, you want a significant amount of time to elapse before you reach significant levels of commitment, physical intimacy, or emotional intimacy.

If some of those four aspects increases significantly faster (or slower) than the others, don't freak out. Just take deliberate action to bring all four back into balance.

In other words, if one side is growing too fast, slow it down. If it's growing too slow, speed it up. Simple, right?

"Slow and Steady" in Practice

I'll admit, this is not a perfect rule.

In a real relationship these four sides will never move at exactly the same speed.

But that's ok. Your goal is to keep your relationship more-or-less in balance, not to perfectly adhere to the square.

Basically, use the square as a check-up tool. Every now and then, take some time to think through where your relationship falls on the square.

If you're finding that some of the sides are increasing much faster or slower than the others, then **make deliberate decisions** to bring them more in balance.

For instance, if you find that your emotional intimacy does not seem to be increasing, maybe you and your partner can try having more conversations about personal topics. A good way to achieve this is by visiting the website 36questionsinlove.com – it has 36 questions that inspire great conversations between you and your partner.

Or, if you find that physical intimacy seems to be increasing way faster than everything else, make an agreement with your partner that you'll be more hands-off for the time being. It's not that physical intimacy is wrong – you just don't want to get there too soon.

Make sense?

This is a lot to digest, so it's ok if it's still a little fuzzy right now. In the next section, I'll explain in detail what I mean by each of the four sides, and how to tell if a side is increasing too fast or too slow.

With that advice under your belt, you'll be fully equipped to apply the "Slow and Steady" squares. Let's go!

<u>Slow and Steady...</u>

Ok. You want your relationship to grow at a healthy rate. And you (mostly) get the idea of the "Slow and Steady" square – it makes sense that time, commitment, physical intimacy and emotional intimacy should go up at the same rate.

But you're probably still left with a lot of questions.

How do you actually figure out how fast those four sides are going up, relative to each other?

How much time do you need before the commitment of boyfriend and girlfriend? How much emotional intimacy do you need before that first kiss?

And what do I mean by all these terms anyway?

Fortunately, the answers to those questions are what we'll address next as we unpack each of the "sides" in turn. In this section, we'll tackle time and commitment, and in part two, we'll discuss emotional and physical and intimacy.

Time

This is the easiest concept to explain, but can be the hardest one to apply. As we've already discussed, relationships need time to grow in a healthy way.

The problem is, how much time?

How soon before your first kiss? How soon before you can share that big secret with them?

There's obviously no one right answer for this. It might be ok for one person to have their first kiss on their first date, whereas someone else might choose to wait until their wedding day for their first kiss.

But if you're committed to asking the question of "Are we going too fast?" you will often find the right answer for you. Just trust your gut.

Or to be more direct, **if you feel that you might be going too fast, you probably are.**

Slow down.

My friend Scott unintentionally gave me some of the best relationship advice I've ever received. We were baking cookies and he said "I always like to check them a few minutes before they're done, just in case. You can always cook them more, but you can never uncook something."

You can't "uncook" a relationship.

But if you take things slow, it's easy to take the brakes off once a little time has passed and you're sure that you're ready for that next step.

So **if you're not sure, slow down.**

It's ok to just enjoy the stage of the relationship that you're in. You don't have to zoom to the next level of intimacy right away.

Commitment

Commitment is the side of the relationship that signals "We're in this for the long haul."

Formal relationship stages are a big part of commitment. Becoming boyfriend and girlfriend, becoming engaged, getting married, etc., are all stages of commitment.

But sometimes commitment takes a more subtle form.

Moving to a different state to be with the person you're dating is a big commitment. Signing up for couple's counseling is a sign of commitment. So is choosing to forgive instead of walking out when you've been hurt.

Take a look at all the ways you are committed to someone – not just what your Facebook relationship status says.

Also, make sure that your commitment grows in pace with everything else. If you're still in the early stages of the relationship with someone, you shouldn't be making long-term commitments because you don't yet know if you're going to be together long-term.

And if you've been with someone for a long time, something is probably amiss if you're not willing to make a commitment to them that reflects the length of your relationship.

In other words, your commitment to the other person should reflect the stage your relationship is currently at. If your commitment to them is way more or less than your intimacy and shared history with them, then something is probably wrong.

Intimacy

Following me so far? Sweet.

Next, we'll explore the final two sides of the "Slow and Steady" Square: emotional and physical intimacy.

Intimacy can be harder to measure than commitment or time. Gauging your intimacy level is much tougher than checking how long you've been dating, or your current stage of commitment.

But intimacy is super important, so I've made sure that the next section will prepare you to grow intimacy in your relationship in a healthy way.

...Wins Their Heart

We've discussed time and commitment – the first two sides of the "Slow and Steady" Square. Now, let's dig into physical and emotional intimacy.

Physical Intimacy

There's nothing wrong about physical intimacy with your partner – provided you go about it in the right way.

Physical intimacy feels good, and if you're attracted to someone it's natural to want to get physical with them.

But physical intimacy is designed to be an expression of emotional intimacy. Doing something physical without an emotional connection feels good in the moment, but it can ultimately lead to feelings of emptiness and loneliness.

Plus, too much physical intimacy too soon can cheapen the emotional intimacy of a relationship. You want your feelings of love and affection towards your partner to be based in who they are and how much you care about them – not based in how nice it feels when you are physical with them. One of the easiest ways to "burn the turkey" when it comes to relationships is to get really physical, really fast.

So when is it ok to start being physical with your partner?

Again, this answer will vary for different couples. But there's a three-step process you can follow to figure out the right answer for you.

First, check your motives for wanting to get physical. Are you more excited about the thought of all of the fun sensations, or are you more excited about the thought of sharing a special kind of intimacy with your partner? Be brutally honest here. If you're more excited about the physical sensations, wait.

Second, take stock of where you are at commitment-wise. Are you still in the very early stages of commitment? Then your level of physical intimacy should probably be very mild. Are you in a later stage of the relationship? Then you can think about introducing a deeper level of physical intimacy.

Third, make your decision about reaching a new level of physical intimacy when you're calm, happy, and not with your partner. 11:30 PM when you're snuggling on the couch is not a good setting for making a wise decision about physical intimacy.

If you're curious, my rule of thumb for my own relationships is that I need to wait on cuddling until I've started dating the girl, I need to wait on kissing until we're boyfriend and girlfriend, I need to wait on intense kissing (i.e., making out) until we've been boyfriend and girlfriend for a while, and I need to wait on sex until marriage.

These boundaries might be different for you, but **pick boundaries and stick to them.** And make sure you know your partner's boundaries, and stick to those, too.

It's fine if you are ready for something at a different stage than me, but make sure you are actually ready. If you jump into physical intimacy too soon, you can't "uncook" that.

Emotional Intimacy

Emotional intimacy is both the easiest and the hardest relationship aspect to describe.

How close do you feel to your partner? How much do you trust them? How well do you know them?

These are easy questions to understand, but are often hard to answer. Feelings are not easily quantified.

The solution is to spend the time you need getting in touch with your feelings. Relationships kick up a maelstrom of emotion – excitement, nervousness, jealousy, joy, all mingled together. It takes time and deliberate work to sort through those feelings.

Are you nervous because this is your first relationship and you don't want to mess up, or are you nervous because you're sensing something wrong? Are you excited to be with this person because you really do feel close to them, or because you just like having someone to hold?

Spend the time it takes to sort through these feelings, in whatever way you process emotion best. Journal or talk with a friend or go for a run. Figure out how you are really feeling about the person you are dating.

It might not happen overnight, but the understanding will come if you keep pursuing it.

You still might not be able to quantify exactly how close you feel. But if your emotional intimacy is at a healthy place, you'll feel a growing sense of peace and contentedness—a sense that everything is ok, and you can rest.

And if things are unhealthy, you'll feel a growing sense of disquiet and concern—and that's a sign that something is not right, and you should find out what's wrong.

Living Your Love Story

Congratulations! You've nearly finished the dating guide.

You haven't learned how to magically cause people to fall in love with you. Nor have I given you foolproof pickup lines, secret clues that someone is interested in you, or any of the other sneaky tricks that fill many dating guides.

What you have learned is how to have an incredible love story.

Because honestly, love is not about tricks. Love, in fact, is about finding a place where you don't need tricks or suave moves or anything other than just being yourself.

It's about being with someone who loves you and accepts you as you are – it's about being with someone who says "I love you for who you are, not for what you can do for me."

And sneaky tricks won't get you there. You arrive at that place through commitment and knowledge – commitment to a healthy relationship, and knowledge of how to get there.

I wrote the guide to share the knowledge I've learned with you. You now know how to recognize a healthy and unhealthy relationship, how to start a relationship in a healthy way, and how to grow your relationship at a healthy pace.

The next step is up to you.

I guarantee that you will be offered shortcuts and compromises. You'll be given the opportunity to sacrifice the long-term good of your partner in exchange for short-term pleasure, and in the moment it might be really tempting.

But you are stronger than that.

Choose interdependence over selfishness. Choose the slow and steady rush over the 1000 degree burnt turkey. Choose to work for a relationship where you can honestly say "I've done everything possible to make my beloved really happy, and I helped them grow into the person they were meant to be."

Will you commit to healthy relationship? I promise you that if you do, you might need to work harder at the beginning. But the sacrifice will be far outweighed by the lifetime of joy and incredible intimacy that you will find waiting for you.

Dating FAQ

How do I know when someone wants to kiss me?

As a general rule, someone who is making a "kiss me" face will find their eyes drawn to your lips. So you'll see them looking at you, and then down at your lips, and then back up to you. They might also be blushing, smiling, or moving closer. It's also common for people to lick or bite their lips.

That being said, you can't know if someone wants to kiss you unless you ask them. Maybe they're looking at your lips because they want to kiss you, or maybe they want to kiss you but they're not ready yet, or maybe they just got tired of making eye contact. So you should always ask. You don't have to make a big deal of it -- just say "Can I kiss your?" If they want to kiss you, you'll get a heartfelt "Yes!" And if they say no, then by asking you avoided the intense awkwardness of trying to kiss someone who didn't want to be kissed.

Also -- if someone doesn't want to kiss you, that's okay. Nobody owes you a kiss. Even if they've kissed you before, they have the right to say no. This is consent 110, and it goes for every kind of physical intimacy, not just kissing.

I hear that the "pick-up artist" scene has lots of tricks to get anyone to fall for you. Should I follow their advice?"

No. For one thing, a lot of pick-up artist advice is very bad. As in, it just won't work, or it will only work if you are naturally charismatic or very lucky.

For another thing, pick-up artist advice poisons intimacy. Instead of teaching you how to form a genuine connection with a partner, they show you cheap tricks that are based on deception. The only relationship that will really satisfy you is a relationship in which you can be your real self, not a relationship where you need to hide behind deception and manipulation.

Finally, it's super unethical. Don't sell your soul to get short-term social success.

How can I be a good kisser?

Ask your partner.

I know, I know, this sounds like a cop out. But the fact is that different people enjoy being kissed in different ways. There's no specific technique I can technique that everyone will like. So ask your partner how they like to be kissed. If they're not sure, try different things and ask for feedback. Make sure they feel comfortable to tell you "I really didn't like that" or "I really like that -- do that more!"

However, there is one guaranteed way to be a better kisser: Good oral hygiene.

I know this doesn't sound very glamorous, but trust me. It's not fun to kiss someone who has bad breath. So start flossing and using mouthwash regularly. Not only will you save on dentist visits, but your kissing partners will thank you.

Where should I take someone for a first date?

Honestly, my preferred first date is usually just dinner or coffee. If I can't enjoy sitting and talking with someone for an hour, I'm not going to enjoy dating them. And if dinner or coffee goes well, then it's easy to plan a more involved date for next time.

Of course, it's okay if you do more than just sitting and talking on your first date. I had one date where I met a girl for dinner, and then we visited a planetarium afterwards for a star show -- so it was a good combination of talking and an activity. But we did enjoy the planetarium more because we got to know each other at dinner first, so I do recommend that you begin your date with something that allows you to sit and talk.

How should I behave on a first date?

Don't try to impress your date. Instead, you have two goals. Have fun, and try to understand your date. Not only will this help you get a good idea if your date would be a good long-term partner, but you will probably end up impressing your date more by trying to understand them than you would if you tried to show off.

I mean, think about it. Who would you be more interested in -- someone who brags about themselves, or someone who asks you insightful, thoughtful questions about yourself?

What are some creative date ideas?

A few dates that have worked well for me:

- Planetariums (especially if you can see a star show!)

- Museums

- Zoos

- The mall!

- Trampoline parks

- Buying coloring books or arts and crafts supplies and having a Kindergarten art day

- Research the local attractions in your area, and visit one you've never been to.

- Visiting a local poetry slam or a concert

- (You might be noticing a theme here -- my dates focus more on fun activities to do together than super romantic locations. This is because the romance will happen naturally if you are having fun together.)

How do I know if I'm ready to date?

That's a good question. If you're dealing with serious mental health issues, or if you're still recovering from a breakup, you probably should get some therapy before you think about a new relationship. If you don't really have any good friends, you should probably try to form some friendships before you pursue a dating relationship. If you have a history of abuse or trauma, you might need to do some healing so that you're not at risk of attracting an abusive partner. And if you're so busy that you don't have the time to invest in another person, then you should probably wait until your schedule clears up.

However, it's different for every person, so your situation is unique. If you're not sure if you're ready for dating, I recommend you talk to a counselor or a trusted friend and get some advice.

How do I ask someone out?

Well, if you don't know them very well, I would encourage saying something like, "Hey, I'd like to get to know you better. Want to get lunch this Friday?" or "Hey, I'm going to a concert this Saturday. Do you want to come?" Basically, if you don't know someone very well, then you shouldn't be romantic out of the gate. Try to spend a little time with them just as friends, so you can get to know them better. This prevents a lot of problems (such as you dating someone and then discovering that you have nothing in common.)

If you've gotten to know someone reasonably well and you're ready to show romantic interest, I recommend being clear but not making a big deal out of it. Say something like "Hey, I think I like you, and

I'd love to take you on a date. Would you like to see a movie this Friday?" By being clear like this, you make it easy for the other person to say yes if they're interested, or say no if they're not (which is a bummer, but it's better to know sooner rather than later.) And by not making it a big deal, you don't make them feel pressured to say yes.

So in other words: If you don't really know someone, don't ask them out romantically, ask them out in a friendly way. After you've spent some time together as friends, then ask them out in a way that is clearly romantic.

Who should I pick to date?

I mean, it should be someone who wants to date you, too.

It should be someone you find at least reasonably attractive, someone who has healthy ways of communicating and handling conflicts, and someone who is compatible with you on your core values and beliefs. It should be someone who cares about you, someone who you trust, and someone who will keep your best interests in mind even if they're angry with you or they've had a bad day.

Beyond that, it should be someone who passes the Forgettable Wednesday Test and the Traffic Test. Both of those terms are from a post on WaitButWhy.com called "How To Choose Your Life Partner Part 2" if you want to read more in depth. Essentially, it should be someone that you enjoy being with even if nothing exciting is going on. Attraction fades, and it eventually becomes less exciting to hold hands or buy someone flowers. But if you have a solid relationship where you just enjoy each other's company, no matter what, then you have a stable foundation to build a relationship on.

Of course, you probably won't know any of this at first. So just go on some dates and see what happens

Once I date someone, all of my problems will be solved, right?

Sorry, but no. Even if you are dating a great partner, you will still struggle with loneliness, sadness, boredom, etc. A romantic relationship is a really positive thing, but it won't magically make your life perfect.

So don't wait until you're dating someone to improve your life. If you're lonely, try to make some friends. If you're sad, talk to a counselor. If you're bored, start a new hobby. Don't wait for a partner to fix you.

How do I make a relationship work long-term?

Honestly, your best bet is to read the book *The Seven Principles for Making Marriage Work* by John Gottman. It's written by a psychologist who has done decades of research on couples, and it's superb. You might also benefit from the book *Crucial Conversations: Tools For Talking When Stakes Are High* by Kerry Patterson and Joseph Grenny. It has the best guide for handling conflict I've ever read, and handling conflict well is one of the biggest skills you need for a successful relationship.

Beyond that, I recommend that you work on yourself. Identify the bad habits that you tend to have in relationships, and work to improve them. Get therapy if you need it, and talk to friends who can help encourage you. It's more fun to try to change your partner, but it's much more effective to try to change yourself.

Chapter 10

How to be a Good Storyteller

People are wired to respond to stories.

There's a reason why so many people flock to the movies or spend hours reading novels – it's because we love to get lost in a good story. And if you ever listen to a good conversation, you'll notice that a lot of connection happens when people share stories with each other.

Unfortunately, there are good ways and bad ways to tell stories – and if you tell stories poorly, you'll lose your audience's interest. So how do you tell a good story during conversations?

Well first we need to define – what makes a story a good story? I'd argue the definition of a good story is very simple:

A good story holds the listeners' interest, builds feelings of connection between narrator and audience, and provides a satisfying conclusion

In other words, these are the three ingredients to a good story:

1) Holding Interest

2) Building Connection

3) Providing a Satisfying Conclusion.

I've got lots of advice for mastering each of the three ingredients. Let's dive in!

Hold Their Interest

- Start With a Hook
- Have a Point to the Story
- Choose the Right Time to Tell The Story
- Show; Don't Tell
- Use Vivid Details, Not Lots of Facts
- Practice Related Skills

Build a Connection

- Tell Personal Stories, but Cautiously
- Share Firsthand Thoughts & Feelings

Provide a Satisfying Conclusion

- When You Get to the End, Stop
- Don't Forget to Pass the Spotlight
- Application & Practice

Holding Interest

Start with a Hook

In order to hold your audience's interest, **you have to get their interest in the first place**. That's why you start with the hook.

A hook is a statement that catches your audience's attention and also clues them in to what's coming up in the story. Let me illustrate with a story that shows how powerful hooks can be (and yes, I just used a hook on you!)

Years ago, psychologists ran an experiment. They asked people to read the following paragraphs:

> *"The procedure is actually quite simple. First you arrange things into different groups. Of course, one pile may be sufficient depending on how much there is to do. If you have to go somewhere else due to lack of facilities that is the next step, otherwise you are pretty well set. It is important not to overdo things. That is, it is better to do too few things at once than too many. In the short run this may not seem important but complications can easily arise. A mistake can be expensive as well. At first the whole procedure will seem complicated.*
>
> *Soon, however, it will become just another facet of life. It is difficult to foresee any end to the necessity for this task in the immediate future, but then one never can tell, After the procedure is completed one arranges the materials into different groups again. Then they can be put into their appropriate places. Eventually they will be used once more and the whole cycle will then have to be repeated. However, that is part of life."*

If you're scratching your head after reading this paragraph, you're not alone – the study participants thought it was goobleygook.

Or well, most of them did. One group of participants was told **"You're about to read some instructions for doing laundry."** For those participants, it was a snap to follow along with the paragraphs (and indeed, if you re-read it now, you'll probably understand what you're hearing much better.)

What does this have to do with storytelling? Simple. If you launch right into a story without giving some context, then **people won't know what to do with the details you're giving them.** It's kind of like giving someone driving directions before they know the starting address. But if you help them understand what your story is about before it beings, they will follow along with no problem.

So offer a hook. Begin a story with something like, "That reminds me of my worst date ever," or "Did I ever tell you about the time I went on a date with a professional wrestler?" **Give people a sense of what the story is about so they don't get lost**. This is especially important for longer stories – if your story is only a few sentences long a hook may not be necessary, but if you're asking people to pay attention to you for 30 seconds or more, you'd better give them a hook.

The other benefit of the hook – if your audience doesn't "bite", then you know not to bore them with the story. If you share a hook and nobody seems interested, you may want to consider telling an abbreviated version of the story, or sharing a different story instead.

Have a Point

Before you tell a story, ask yourself **"Why would my audience want to hear this story?"**

Is it because the story is funny? Exciting? Touching? Interesting? What emotional response is your story likely to elicit from your listeners? (If you can't come up with an answer to this question, this might be a sign you should find a better topic for your story!)

The reason you ask this question is so that you can choose your details carefully, to make sure they support this goal. If you're at the grocery store preparing to bake a cake, you don't load your shopping cart with fish and jalapeños because those ingredients don't help you bake a cake. Similarly, you want to pack your story with only details that support the goal of the story.

In other words, if you are telling a funny story, get to the funny stuff as soon as possible – don't waste time giving boring details. If you are telling a touching story, your goal is to tug on your audience's heartstrings, so be more careful when using humorous details. If you're trying to make an exciting story, then your goal should be to build momentum and suspense, so you shouldn't include details that sacrifice momentum.

For example: Let's say I want to tell a funny story about an experience in Mexico. Here are two versions – see which one you like better.

Version One:

> *"When I was in Mexico, I decided to go to a club with some friends. We first met up at someone's house, and we spent some time sitting around and talking. Then, we walked to the club, but decided we were hungry, so we stopped on the way at a Mexico 7-11 and bought some Cheetos. Except in Mexico, they call them "Chetos" for some reason. After we ate our Cheetos, we went into the club. It was really loud, but everyone seemed like they were having fun. We danced for a while, and then I noticed that a guy in a bear costume came onto the dance floor. He started a conga line, and a bunch of people went on the conga line after him. They congaed right off the dance floor and into another room and I never saw any of them again. To this day, I wonder if the bear costume guy was secretly a kidnapper, and he lured the group away to abduct them!"*

Version Two:

> *"When I was in Mexico, I decided to go to a club with some friends. I was dancing, and then I looked up and I saw a guy in a bear costume! He started a conga line, and a bunch of people joined up and congaed right off the dance floor with him, into another room. I never saw any of them again, and to this day I wonder if the bear costume guy was secretly a kidnapper who lured the dancers away to abduct them."*

Most likely, you liked version two better. Why? Because it got to the punchline – the dancing kidnapper bear – much faster! All of the details about meeting at the friend's house, the Cheetos, etc. were all true – but they were irrelevant.

The point was to get to the punchline, so any details that did not support that punchline should be removed. In the first story, by the time I actually got to the punchline, you were probably skimming and wondering "What's the point?" So when the punchline actually arrived, you were not very invested in my story, and you didn't find it very funny.

If you do this right, your conclusion will feel very satisfying to your audience because everything in the story was building to that conclusion. Not only do you maintain their interest as you're telling the story, but you also create the possibility for a really powerful conclusion.

Choose the Right Time

A great story at the wrong time is a terrible story. If you don't believe me, try telling a funny story in the middle of a funeral.

How do you know that it's the right time to tell the story? There's no perfect rule (it's more of an art than a science), but here are a few things to look for:

Don't interrupt another person's story.

People will often introduce their stories with a short statement to get your interest. You are supposed to ask a question in response to this opening statement to launch their story. You are not supposed to tell a story of your own.

For instance, if your friend says, "So the other day I went to the movie theater," he probably wants you to ask him about his trip to the movie theater. He does not want you to jump in and say, "Oh yeah, I was just there last week! I saw the coolest movie; let me tell you all about it...

Avoid interrupting their story before it reaches the "punchline."

If it doesn't seem like the story is finished, wait before you jump in with a story of your own. Instead, ask questions to show interest in the other person's story.

Make sure your story fits the mood of the conversation.

If people are sharing light, funny stories, and you share a chilling ghost story, you'll bring down the mood. Conversely, if people are somberly discussing a recent tragedy, it's not the time to tell the story of your zany Uncle Bob.

Try to make your story relate to something in the conversation.

If everyone is telling travel stories, tell a travel story. If everyone is telling funny stories, share something humorous. The connection doesn't need to be very strong, but other people should be able to tell how your story is connected to the previous conversation.

Make sure your audience has the necessary context to understand the story.

If I tell a story about my friend Greg to an audience that knows Greg, they will probably appreciate the story. But if the audience has never heard of Greg, then I might want to choose another story to tell (or at least, make sure I begin the story by giving a little background on Greg.)

Observe the rest of the group to see when others share stories.

Observing others is a great option, especially if you feel very uncomfortable about sharing. If you spend a little time noticing when other share stories, you will develop an intuition for when it's appropriate to share your own story. Don't stay on the sidelines forever, but it's okay to wait and observe sometimes if needed.

Show, Don't Tell

"Show; don't tell" is the cardinal rule of writing, and it's true for telling stories too.

Telling is when you say something like, "And then, he did the funniest dance – it was so hilarious." **It's *telling* because I can't imagine what you're describing, so your words don't inspire an emotional response in me**. You told me the dance was funny, but it doesn't feel funny to me as the listener.

But if you say something like, "And then he waved his hands above his heads, and gave these short, stiff jumps like he was popcorn being popped," now you're *showing* – and that means that I'm much more likely to be able to tap into the humor of what you're describing. I can imagine the scene in my head and that imagined scene is almost as funny as being there in person.

In other words, *showing* is when you give me everything I need to imagine the scene.

Unfortunately, this creates a problem. Showing takes time, and if you show every little thing that happens in your story, the story will quickly get long-winded. So what's the solution?

Simple. **Show only the scenes or details that matter to your story.**

If you are telling the story of how you survived a shark attack, you don't need to "show" how relaxing the water was before the shark attacked – but you had better show how you dramatically fought off the shark!

Also, make sure you don't repeat details. If you're telling the story about how you talked with a super cute girl, it's natural to mention how good she looked over and over – but it's not interesting for your audience. Your audience will be tempted to tune you out unless you keep serving them interesting new details.

The bottom line: share a detail once (twice, tops) and then move on to something new. If you repeat details, you'll easily stray from showing into telling.

Use Vivid Details, Not Lots of Facts

If you're a witness talking to the police, then it's great for you to offer facts on everything that you remember.

If you're telling a story, not so much. Adding too many details and descriptions is a surefire way to bore your audience.

However, you still need to add some details. So how do you add enough details to keep the story interesting, without overloading your audience? The answer is to use vivid details. Vivid details stand out in your listeners' minds and really help your audience imagine the scene.

What makes a detail vivid? A few things:

Vivid details are surprising.

If I tell you that a lawyer in court is wearing a suit, that's not surprising – since most people in court wear suits. However, if someone goes to the beach wearing a suit, now that detail becomes vivid and interesting.

Vivid details relate to the story.

If I'm telling you a story about spilling a soda on my date in the movie theater, I don't really need to give details about the movie itself – since the story is about my embarrassing spill, not the movie.

Vivid details help the reader imagine the scene.

If you tell me the train was "very fast" I can't really imagine that. If you tell me, "The train was going so fast everything outside was a blur," now you've given me something to imagine.

Vivid details are important.

If I'm telling a story about meeting the president, it doesn't really matter what color tie the president was wearing – since the important thing is the meeting, not the tie! However, if you met the president and you happened to be wearing the exact same tie as him that would perhaps be an important detail.

Also, remember the earlier rule: make sure everything supports the "point" of the story. If your detail doesn't support the point of the story, it probably doesn't need to be included.

Practice Related Skills

Of course, the best way to practice storytelling is to tell stories in conversation.

But there are other great ways that you can build your storytelling skills.

Improv theater is a great option. Improv theater can help you improve all kinds of social skills, but it's especially great for storytelling because it forces you to trust your instinct, and it gives you a great perception for what makes a good story. If you live in a major city, there is probably an improv theater class near you (and even if you're in a small town, it's worth checking.)

Toastmasters is another good option. Although Toastmasters focuses on public speaking, not storytelling, most good speeches have a few stories in them. Do a few months of Toastmasters, and you'll feel much more comfortable having an audience's attention, and your storytelling skills will sharpen as well.

Finally, try writing stories! Find some websites that offer writing prompts, and try to write them. A good rule of thumb is to try to write "flash fiction", which is a story that has 500 words or less.

Writing a story in 500 words or less is great practice for conversational storytelling, since most of your stories that you tell in conversation won't be longer than 500 words. Although flash fiction has "fiction" in the name, you don't need to write made-up stories — it's fine to practice by writing down stories from your life.

Got writer's block? Try Googling for "flash fiction prompts!"

As you write, don't worry too much about good writing – worry about good storytelling. (You may even want to give yourself a time limit for each story so you practice telling the story, not editing it.) There's no need to try for symbolism or fancy wordplay – instead, just write a story that people would want to read.

Building Connections

Tell Personal Stories, but Cautiously

There's nothing wrong with telling a story about crazy Uncle Jim or the kind old lady who lives down the street.

But when you tell stories about other people, the potential for connection is limited. It's only when you tell a personal story about your own life that you create the greatest opportunity to connect with others.

So tell stories about your own life! They don't have to be dramatic or monumental. Your audience might enjoy hearing about the games you played with your childhood friends, or the drama team you were on in college, or the new ballet classes you just started taking. **If your story is about something that is important to YOU, there's a decent chance it will be interesting to your audience.** Plus, stories from your life allow your audience to learn something new about you, which builds connection.

Also, you have many more memories to draw on when you tell a story from your life. If you're telling a secondhand story you heard from someone else, you probably don't remember many details, and it will be much harder to make the story interesting. But if your story is about something that happened to you, then you can draw from your memory banks to fill the story with richness and interesting detail.

That being said, you need to be careful about how much you share. Connection needs to build over time. If you jump right to a very intimate story before connection has had the time to build, it can make your audience uncomfortable.

For instance, let's say you recently had a family member pass away from cancer and you went through a period of depression. If you share the story of their illness and your depression with a casual acquaintance, they might feel uncomfortable because you've shared something very personal with someone you didn't know very well. Conversely, it would be fine to share that story with a group of close friends because they do know you well.

Of course, you don't have to wait until someone is your best friend before sharing personal stories with them. But be extra careful with people you don't know as well.

Start by sharing a semi-personal story and see how they react. If they react positively, then down the road you could share stories that are more personal. If they become uncomfortable, then you can avoid sharing personal stories with that person (at least until you get to know them better.)

Share Firsthand Thoughts and Feelings

When you tell a story about something that happened to you, don't just say what happened. Talk about how you felt and what you were thinking.

In other words, don't limit your story to facts that an outside observer would have noticed. Instead, give your audience a window inside your head by sharing your thoughts and feelings. This will help your audience to experience the story as you did, building connection.

Here's an example.

Bad:

> *"I stood up in front of the class to give a presentation on the War of 1812. I hadn't prepared at all for the presentation, and I didn't know anything about the War of 1812. Just then, the school prankster pulled the fire alarm and we all left class."*

Good:

> *"I stood up in front of the class to give a presentation on the War of 1812. I was incredibly nervous because I hadn't prepared at all for the presentation. I remember feeling so queasy I wondered if I would throw up – and then I remember thinking, "It would be better to throw up then to fail this presentation!" I racked my brain for anything I knew about the War of 1812, when I heard the fire alarm ring. This feeling of absolute bliss welled up inside me as I left the class, and I remember having the biggest smile on my face for the rest of the day."*

Both stories are about the same events, but one story is rather bland, whereas the other story lets you get to know the narrator a little bit. When you tell your stories, give your audience a window inside your head, and they'll feel more connected to you.

A Satisfying Conclusion

Stop When You Reach the End

The easiest way to tell a bad story is to tell a good story, and then keep going after you should have stopped.

Once your story reaches the climax – the punchline of a funny story, the creative solution in a story about solving a problem, the moment of greatest emotional impact in a touching story – you should try to bring it to an ending as quickly as possible. In other words, **when you reach the end, stop!**

Obviously, you don't need to end the story abruptly as soon as you say the climax – it's okay to have a little resolution. But your natural temptation if you've told a good story is to keep talking, because everyone will be paying attention to you and attention feels good. Resist that temptation.

When the story is done, stop talking. Don't give minor details, or summarize the story. And for goodness sake, don't launch immediately into another story – give someone else the floor.

Good:

> "...And when he got back from the hospital, he found that the entire office had come together to raise money to pay for his treatment."

Bad:

> "...And when he got back from the hospital, he found that the entire office had come together to raise money to pay for his treatment. It was such a touching and heartwarming moment. The office really supported him in that moment, and he felt like everything was going to be okay. I mean, can you believe how generous the office was to pay for his treatment?"

Really Bad:

> *"...And when he got back from the hospital, he found that the entire office had come together to raise money to pay for his treatment. It was such a touching and heartwarming moment. The office really supported him in that moment, and he felt like everything was going to be okay. I mean, can you believe how generous the office was to pay for his treatment? And by the way, that reminds me of another story..."*

In some cases, your story might not have a climax. Perhaps you're telling a story about what you did on your vacation to Europe, and while you have many interesting memories to share, there's not a single memory that works as the "climax."

In that case, just wrap up your story in a deliberate way. That will signal to everyone that you are done speaking. For instance, you might conclude a story about your European vacation by saying. "Gosh, it's overwhelming how many memories we have from that trip. Even though we enjoyed it, I'm definitely happy to be home and sleeping in my own bed again."

Your audience is not expecting your wrap-up to be brilliant or compelling. As long as your story finishes in a deliberate way instead of just trailing off, you should be fine.

Pass the Spotlight

Okay, you've just told your story, and it went great. Your audience was interested the whole time, and you gave them a great conclusion. Time to tell another story, right?

Wrong.

Storytelling works best when everyone gets a turn. Groups get a particular kind of energy when great storytelling is happening – each person builds off the person before them, and the story I told inspires the story you are about to tell. It's a great experience that is much harder to achieve when just one person is telling the stories.

So be gracious. Pass the attention to someone else. This might be subtle – just pausing for a few seconds to let someone else jump in. Or this might be more direct – perhaps you ask the group, "Does anyone else have any childhood stories to share?"

You might even invite someone directly to share a story. For instance: "Jose, didn't you go to Disneyland last week? Want to share some stories from that trip?"

Inviting someone directly is especially useful for making others feel included, and for helping shyer members of the group get a chance to share.

Of course, you're not limited to one story per conversation. Just let one or two others share before you tell another story. The rest of the group will appreciate the opportunity to share, and the group conversation will be more satisfying for everyone.

Application and Practice

If you want to be a good storyteller in conversation, you need to hold your audience's interest, provide your audience with a satisfying conclusion, and look for opportunities to connect with your audience.

You also need to practice. The best place to start practicing is by writing stories down. That way, you can practice in private, and you can also read through your stories afterwards to critique yourself. (You can also record yourself speaking and listen to the recordings.)

When practicing a story, don't worry about getting it perfect. Each story should only take you 1-3 minutes to tell, so avoid spending a ton of time on each story. And since you're practicing your storytelling technique, not your writing technique, don't worry about things like spelling or word choice.

Storytelling

These are some ideas to get you started. Do your best to write a story for each of these experiences. Once you've written about each one of these ideas, try to come up with your own ideas for stories you can tell!

Tell a story about...

- A childhood memory

- Learning a new skill

- A time you felt really happy

- A funny mistake you made

- Your first day at a new job

- Discovering a new hobby

- A time when you were really proud of yourself

Once you've practiced writing stories down and you feel confident, it's time to practice telling stories in conversation. When in conversation, look for an opportunity to share a relevant story. To start with, try to share short (30 seconds or less) stories. As you have success with shorter stories, try longer stories.

Of course, this requires consistency. If you practice storytelling once a month, you're unlikely to get better. So be deliberate to build in several opportunities to practice each week.

Over time, you'll find your storytelling skill gets better and better. Keep practicing, and you'll be a storytelling expert before you know it!

Chapter 11
Best Blog Posts

On ImproveYourSocialSkills.com, I've been writing blog posts since 2012. Here are a few of my favorite ones.

Better Every Day

So my work just unveiled a new slogan: "Better Every Day."

Normally, company slogans are pretty bland. But there's a powerful idea here.

Greatness doesn't happen overnight. Most things worth doing take persistence and hard work.

But often, we look for a quick fix and fast results. When we put in some effort and don't see immediate improvement, it's easy to give up or say, "I'll take a break and come back later."

Or, we look at the end goal compared to where we are now, and the distance between them just seems unmanageable. We think, "I'll never be able to get there from here," so we never even try.

But here's the thing.

If you're 1% better every day, you are **38 times better** every year.

And 1% better every day is doable. It means having one conversation that you might have shied away from, or accepting one social invitation you might have declined. It means spending ten minutes reading through a social skills guide instead of a humor site. It means deciding to ask a friend or family member for help, or pick up the phone and schedule that counseling appointment.

Commit to being better every day.

You won't see improvement immediately, but it will come. And when it does, it will be exceptional.

How can you be better today?

IMPROVE YOUR SOCIAL SKILLS

<u>Give it 100</u>

Social skills are like any other skill — **if you practice, you get better.**

But in order to practice, you have to start, and you have to keep going. And both of those things are very hard. It's really easy to wait to start until you're totally "ready" (which will be never), or burn yourself out by pursuing a new goal in an unsustainable way.

So instead, I want to show you a better way.

There's a website called Give it 100. The basic idea is that you practice something for 100 days in a row, and you film a 10 second clip of you doing it every day so you can see how you improve. You can also see what other users are doing, which is sometimes incredible and sometimes adorable.

Unfortunately, social skills don't really lend themselves well to 10 second clips (in fact, a great social skills tip: don't randomly start filming the people you're talking to.) So instead I want to give you a different "Give it 100" challenge. Are you ready? Here it is:

Do something that practices your social skills for ten minutes, ten days in a row.

For instance, you could

- Spend ten minutes reading a guide to social skills

- Spend ten minutes watching TV with the volume off to analyze body language

- Spend ten minutes researching therapists — and then booking an appointment when you find one!

- Spend ten minutes talking to someone you otherwise wouldn't have.

At the end of ten days, you'll have spent 100 minutes improving your social skills. This doesn't sound like a lot, but it's about momentum.

I guarantee that if you "give it 100" you will see an improvement in your social skills and your confidence — even if it's very small (which is ok, because every good thing starts small.)

Once you see that improvement, it will be much easier for you to keep improving, and do another 100, and then another 100 — until you look back and you find that your first 100 minutes of improvement has become 100 hours.

So to summarize:

- Commit to spending 10 minutes over the next 10 days to practice your social skills. If possible, start today — or at the latest, tomorrow.

- Once you've "given it 100", notice the improvement (even if it's small!) in your social skills and confidence

- Then, **keep going!** Give it another 100, or maybe another 1000!

- And come back and post your story on ImproveYourSocialSkills.com to encourage others!

<u>Fight Back</u>

Life is really hard sometimes.

There are times when all of the encouragement in the world doesn't seem to help, times when it feels like the only emotions available are rage or grief or numbness, times when starting another day feels like getting in the ring with Mohammed Ali.

Maybe that's your story today.

Maybe that's been your story for a long time.

If that's you, I want you to know that it will get better. You will not always suffer. You will find healing and you will find people who will love you very much and you will have moments when life will be so good that your heart will feel like dancing right out of your chest. You are not a mistake. You are not a lost cause. It is good that you are alive and **one day you will believe that.**

But I also want to recognize that things might not get better right away. And I know that when people tell me, "This will be better someday, but you just need to wait," I don't find their words very helpful.

So I want to give you more than just waiting.

I want to give you the chance to fight back.

In the olden days, people wrote legends of battles with monsters – dragons and hydras and sphinxes. Today we still have monsters; they just have names like depression and loneliness and addiction. Maybe you are locked in your own hard fight with one of these monsters, and maybe that fight is going to take some time to win.

But **your own fight will help you fight for others.**

Viktor Frankl, a survivor of Nazi concentration camps, said, "In some ways suffering ceases to be suffering at the moment it finds a meaning, such as the meaning of a sacrifice." He found that people who fixated on escaping the camps tended to fall ill and die more easily.

But the people who created a meaning for themselves in the camp – through tending to other prisoners, creating art, or simply maintaining their dignity in the face of incredible suffering – were more likely to survive and even find moments of joy. Frankl said, "Those who have a 'why' to live can bear almost any 'how.'"

If you've forgotten your 'why', I want you to find it. I want you to remember that you matter very much, and it is very good that you are alive and that your life has meaning.

And I want you to know that **your suffering can have meaning**, if you let it.

For me, my suffering taught me how to love other people better. My childhood of social rejection taught me to reach out to others on the outskirts – and eventually to write a social skills guide that helps readers find community. For one of my friends, surviving abuse led her into a career where she could help protect others. Another friend fills her writing with the healing wisdom that she learned from her pain.

For you, maybe your suffering will equip you to reach out to others who are suffering in a similar way. Maybe you will create art or music or writing that is beautiful and life-giving, because your suffering has taught you how to touch the deep places in a person's soul. Maybe someone will stay alive because you can sit with them and say, **"I know what you're going through."**

Henri Nouwen once wrote, "The great illusion of leadership is to think that man can be led out of the desert by someone who has never been there."

Maybe today you are in a desert, and it feels like the sand will never end. You don't deserve that, and I don't know why sometimes it takes so long for things to get better.

But I do know that even if you can't leave your desert yet, **you can be an oasis to someone in their own desert.** I know that your words and your love and your presence have the potential to heal and to bring joy to others. And I hope that when you see your power to bring light into the life of others, some light will enter your life too.

I'm not saying that you should take care of others instead of taking care of yourself. But I am saying that **your suffering is not meaningless, just as your life is not meaningless.** Your suffering will teach you to love better, to create art that is truer and more beautiful, to be an agent of healing and light for people who are desperate for both.

For wanderers lost in a thirsty desert, you will provide relief and encouragement.

For weary warriors locked in battle with a fierce monster, you will be a stalwart comrade-in-arms.

And as you fight for others, **you will find that you are worth fighting for, too.**

<u>Take Care of Yourself and Others</u>

Would you climb a mountain with a backpack full of rocks?

You would probably stop and remove the rocks first — even if this means you don't start your climb right away. Or, if you couldn't remove the rocks, you would still understand that you don't need to climb as fast as someone who isn't weighed down.

For some reason, we don't apply this same logic to self-improvement.

We might be weighed down by social anxiety, or past trauma, or an empty bank account, or problems with physical or mental health, or by a schedule that is jam packed with commitments — the rocks that we carry can look very different.

But our response to them is unfortunately very similar. Either we try to ignore them and push ourselves towards incredibly ambitious goals (and then pay the cost in burnout and shame when our burdens block us from those goals), or we give up and say, "I can't even try to climb this mountain — my rocks are too heavy."

I'd like to propose a different way.

Instead of surrendering to our burdens or trying to ignore them, **let's try to take care of ourselves.**

Maybe that means spending more time doing the things that you love, even if it feels like a waste of time.

Maybe that means reaching out to a counselor or a friend and letting them know you're struggling.

Maybe that means saying, "No," to some things in your life.

Maybe it just means giving yourself permission to not be ok all the time.

Don't get me wrong — I'm all about self-improvement. **But sometimes you need to take care of yourself before you can improve yourself.**

So my challenge for you is simple. Figure out how you could take the first step towards removing some rocks — or at least towards accepting yourself, rocks and all — and then go do it.

The Case for Small Talk

Lots of people tell me, "I hate small talk."

And in truth, small talk can be tiresome sometimes. When you're discussing a topic you don't care about, it's natural to get bored.

Small talk can be doubly frustrating when you've craving deep interactions. After you've experienced true heart-to-heart conversation, how can you go back to discussing the weather?

It's understandable to feel like small talk is a waste of time – the "busywork" of social interaction.

Understandable – but wrong.

Small talk has huge potential to help you connect with others. Let's look at the three reasons why:

1) Small Talk Prepares You for Connection

Just like stretching helps prepare your muscles for exercise, **small talk helps prepare people for intimacy**.

When you make small talk with someone, you give them the opportunity to get used to you and to settle into the conversation.

Moreover, people expect deeper conversations to be preceded by small talk. Even if you are comfortable skipping straight to the "meat" of the conversation, it will throw others for a loop. It's kind of like shaking hands when you meet someone – if you don't do it when they expect it, it comes across as weird.

2) Small Talk Communicates Interest.

With small talk, what you communicate is more important than what you say.

If you say something insignificant like, "What do you think of the weather?" you are communicating that you want to hear my thoughts. When you crack a lame joke, you are communicating that you want to make me laugh. All of these things communicate that you like me and you want to get to know me better.

This is important because it paves the way for deeper interaction. Deeper interaction involves risk. If I share my personal beliefs with you, I risk you starting an argument with me. If I share a personal struggle, I risk you responding with cruel callousness. So I need to know it's safe before I go deeper.

When you communicate interest, you communicate safety. You communicate, "I care about what you have to say, and I'm open to you sharing it." Obviously, this isn't a perfect guarantee – sometimes people will be very pleasant in small talk and still respond poorly when the conversation goes deeper. But in general, when you show interest during small talk, you help people feel comfortable going deeper with you.

3) Small Talk Establishes Common Ground

Small talk lets you discover what you have in common.

You can find the topics that get both of you excited, the parts of your stories that you're eager to share. This will naturally lead the conversation into paths that are more intimate and meaningful.

Not only does this give you fuel for more conversation, but it also helps you form bonds with the other person. When you discover common ground, you start to imagine life through the other person's eyes. As the author Donald Miller says, small talk lets us ask, "What do we have in common, so I can understand you through the lens of my own experience?"

While deep heart-to-heart conversations are very intimate, small talk can be intimate too. Heartfelt friendships will begin to form even before the first deep conversation – because small talk allowed the friends to discover how much they resonate with each other.

The Value of Small Talk

If small talk feels like busywork, you're missing the big picture.

Instead of treating small talk like a chore you have to get through, make small talk an opportunity to make a connection. When you begin small talk, ask yourself:

- How can I help the other person feel comfortable?

- How can I communicate interest and friendliness?

- How can I discover common ground?

Let these questions guide you, and you'll find big value in small talk.

3 Hobbies that Teach Social Skills

Social skills improve with practice. The more time you spend interacting with others, the better you become at social interaction. (Makes sense, right?)

Unfortunately, finding the opportunity to practice can be difficult. If you want to be a better runner, you can lace on your shoes and run around the block, but if you want to get better at social skills, where do you go to practice?

That's what this article is all about. Sit tight, and I'll tell you three of my favorite hobbies that helped me improve my social skills – and that can help you, too!

1) Improv Theater

In improv(isational) theater, everything is made up on the spot. No script, no planning ahead of time. You just go out and make a scene from nothing. The scenes are often hilarious, sometimes poignant, and always entertaining.

As I've noted elsewhere, improv is a lot like social interaction. And the same principles that equip you to feel confident striding on stage and making a scene from nothing will also help you to have confidence and competence in social situations.

And, just like social interaction, improv is for everyone. You don't have to be naturally funny or theatrical. Improv works based on a few simple principles (like accepting and building on what your partner brings to the scene), and any improv class will teach you to apply those principles like a pro.

In an improv class, you start by doing lots of fun games and exercises that help you become comfortable with using your imagination and thinking on your feet, and then you start making some scenes with other students. It's super fun, and you will often make good friends with the other students.

Improv has taught me to have more confidence, think on my feet, and be comfortable when I'm pushed outside my comfort zone. Take a moment and search for improv theater classes in your area – then sign up! You'll be happy you did.

2) Partner Dancing

Partner dancing is a great way to meet people and become more comfortable in your own skin.

I'm not talking about choreographed dancing (although that can be fun too!) Instead, I'm referring to dances like salsa, swing, or ballroom, where you're paired up with someone and you make up the dance as you go along.

Much like improv, anyone can learn partner dancing. There are tons of beginners classes designed for people with no experience, and it doesn't take long to get the basics down. And once you have a few classes under your belt, you'll find that you move with more grace and confidence in your everyday life, which will help you make positive first impressions.

Plus, dancing allows you to meet new people. Many cities have social dancing events, where people go to meet others to dance with. You might dance with a dozen people during the course of the night, which means you get a dozen opportunities to practice conversation, get to know someone else, and make a new friend!

Bottom line: Dancing is a great skill, it's a lot of fun, and it will help you socially. Give it a try!

3) Toastmasters Public Speaking

Toastmasters is a public speaking club that is active in over 100 countries. It is a phenomenal way to overcome social anxiety, get better at public speaking, and learn how to communicate clearly and effectively. I did Toastmasters and loved it – you can see me giving a Toastmasters speech if you search for "Daniel Wendler to live an epic" on Youtube.

You don't need speaking experience to join Toastmasters – most people who join have never given a speech before.

Toastmasters clubs usually meet once a week and follow a simple format. Everyone gets the chance to speak for about a minute at every meeting, by giving an impromptu answer to an interesting question (e.g., "What would you do if you were president?") Then, 2-3 people will give a prepared speech, about a topic that they chose. After that, someone will offer constructive, positive feedback to the people who gave a speech.

Toastmasters works wonders on your social skills because it gives you consistent opportunities to practice and to get good feedback. Instead of practicing blindly, you'll get expert advice from people who want to help you succeed. And you'll have the opportunity to practice every week, so you will improve quickly. There is probably a Toastmasters club near you, so check them out!

Social Skills Hobbies

There you have it – three hobbies that improve your social skills.

All three of these hobbies have helped me in my own life, and I strongly encourage you to give them a try.

Are there any hobbies that have helped you in your social skills journey? Share them on ImproveYourSocialSkills.com!

How to be More Social

If you're reading *Improve Your Social Skills*, it's probably because you want to be more social. You don't study social skills so you can sit in your room alone – you study them so you can go out and be social!

But how do you actually make that happen? And what does "being social" even mean, anyway?

Well, the first step is to spend some time building up your social skills. If you try to be social and then run into trouble because your social skills need work, you're going to get discouraged and it will be harder to be social in the future.

But let's say you've already put in the time to study and practice your social skills, and you feel confident. You've studied how to make conversation, and you've brushed up on your body language. You may not be perfect, but you're ready to put your social skills to use.

If that's you, then becoming more social is easy. Here's how you do it:

Many Roads To Social Success

First, realize that there is no one right way to be social.

"Being social" for you will look different than it does for others, and that's ok.

I have a friend who plays in a different Dungeons and Dragons game almost every night. He dedicates the majority of his social time to these games, but it's a social life that works for him. He gets to spend hours with his friends, doing an activity he enjoys.

I have another friend who goes out dancing 3-4 times per week. Most of her social time is dedicated to meeting new people on the dance floor, and that's the social life that works for her.

I prefer to bounce between a lot of different social activities – my social calendar is always different week to week. That's the social life that works for me.

Find Your Social Rhythm

By now, you've probably realized my point.

"Being social" doesn't mean that you have to hit the bar scene, or go to parties.

"Being social" means that you discover what a rich, fulfilling social life looks like for you, and then live that out.

If you need a long time to rest between social engagements, being social might mean one social event per week. If you thrive on interaction, being social might mean a new event each day.

If you already have a solid group of friends, being social might mean that you spend most of your time with them. Or, it might mean that you split your time between your old friends and opportunities to meet new friends.

In any case, it needs to be something that works for YOU.

Your "Be Social" Blueprint

Of course, you might not know what a rich, fulfilling social life looks like for you. And that's ok.

Like many other areas of life, being social takes time to figure out. But there's an easy two-step process that can help you through it. I call it "Ponder & Go Yonder."

First, **ponder** your social goals and your previous social experiences.

Think through what has worked for you in the past, and what has been flawed in the past that you would like to improve for the future. The goal is not to figure things out completely, but to discover a few possibilities for areas where you can grow your social life.

Second, **go yonder**.

By this I mean try something that is new but achievable. The word "yonder" refers to something that is distant but within view. Try for that balance of "distant but within view" when pondering new ways to be more social.

In other words, explore new social opportunities that may be a bit challenging or scary (i.e., "distant") but make sure they are still achievable (i.e., "within view.")

Growing Towards Social Success

"Ponder & Go Yonder" is a repeating process.

You'll spend some time thinking, which will give you an idea for something new for you to try. That new experience will give you more fuel for thought, and your thinking will in turn lead to new experiences.

The cycle keeps repeating, and every time it does, you grow a little closer to a full understanding of what "being social" looks like for you.

So there's no rush. Just commit to a slow and steady cycling of "Ponder & Go Yonder" and you grow steadily closer to the rich, fulfilling social life you desire.

Making Great First Impressions with the Name Game

People like hearing their names. When you use someone's name, it helps them to feel comfortable, and remembering their name makes it much easier for you to strike up a conversation later on.

Unfortunately, if you want to use someone's name, you need to remember it, and remembering names is hard. Fortunately, remembering names is much easier with **one simple trick**.

I call it **"Playing the name game."**

To play the name game, follow these three rules.

Rule 1: Get Their Name ASAP

When you first meet someone, **get their name within the first few minutes of the conversation**. You can either ask for it directly, or just introduce yourself. Most folks will give you their name when you give them yours. Once you get their name, **repeat it immediately.** If they say "My name is Bob" say "It's great to meet you, Bob" not "It's great to meet you." The early repetition ensures that the name makes it into your short term memory.

Rule 2: Make Their Name Memorable

Now, it's time to move the name into your long-term memory. To do that, **combine the name with a memorable adjective.** A memorable adjective is either an adjective that starts with the same letter as the name, or that rhymes with the name. For instance, "Cool Carl" or "Dan the Man."

Ideally, this adjective should be somewhat related to the person ("Bob from Boston" is great if Bob is actually from Boston), but it doesn't have to be. Any combination that either rhymes or starts with the same letter will do. Repeat this combination to yourself a few times to make sure it fixes in your memory (but make sure you don't say it out loud – Mustache Mike might not appreciate the title you've given him)

Rule 3: Lock Their Name in Your Memory

Then, cement the name/adjective combination in your memory by repeating it mentally a few times during the conversation. This is exactly as simple as it sounds – just think to yourself, "That is Cool Carl," a few times during the conversation. You don't have to keep up a constant repetition in your head – just remind yourself whenever you think of it.

When you follow these three rules, you'll find remembering names are much easier. Getting their name immediately allows you to focus on their name before the conversation takes off and demands more of your attention, and repeating a memorable name/adjective combination will cement their name in your mind for the long term.

Also, one bonus rule: If you forget their name, just make sure you ask again near the end of the conversation. I find that once you've had the chance to get to know someone in a conversation, remembering their name is much easier (because you have some memories to pin the name to.) So if playing the name game at the beginning of the conversation doesn't work for you, just play it at the end. Chances are, they forgot your name too, so they'll appreciate the chance to ask again.

In any case, remembering names will still take work, and you won't remember every name. But play the name game and I guarantee that you have much greater success remembering names.

How to Make Eye Contact

Making good eye contact is tough.

Give too much eye contact, and you come across as too intense (at best) or a staring creeper (at worst).

Give too little eye contact, and the other person might think you don't care about what they have to say.

Plus, when you're worrying about making good eye contact, the rest of the interaction suffers. Instead of enjoying a great conversation, you're stressing about eye contact.

That's not good for anyone.

The Secret of Great Eye Contact

Fortunately, there's a simple trick that will help you master great eye contact.

Just **match your eye contact with your partner's.**

If they look at you, look at them. If they look away, look away.

Easy, right?

Here's why it works. There's no such thing as "perfect" eye contact. Your goal is to make your partner feel comfortable with you, which means all you need to do is avoid giving too much eye contact or not enough.

Different people feel comfortable with different levels of eye contact. But almost everybody will initiate the amount of eye contact that they feel comfortable with. That means that if you give them the same amount of eye contact that they give you, they'll probably feel comfortable.

Look at your partner when they look at you (and look away when they don't), and you'll be squarely inside the level of eye contact they feel comfortable with. It really is that easy.

Mastering Good Eye Contact

Of course, there are a few details to take care of.

You don't want to mirror your partner exactly, or they'll quickly realize you're copying them. It's ok to instantly match their eye contact on occasion, but in general, you should wait a few seconds before copying them. Wait about one second before looking at them, and about two or three seconds before looking away.

Those numbers are just rough guidelines, of course. Feel free to experiment to find what feels natural for you. The important thing is that you **avoid moving like a mirror image of your partner.** The exact timing of your pauses is less important.

Also, be aware that eye contact rules change somewhat when you're having an emotional conversation. It's sometimes easier to discuss emotional issues when you're not looking at someone, so when people are sharing something very personal or emotional, they will sometimes look away from the person they are speaking to.

If that happens, you still need to look at them to show that you care. If your gaze wanders, that communicates that you don't really care about what they're saying, which is bad at any time but especially hurtful when they're sharing something emotional.

Eye Contact Rhythm

As you start to practice matching your partner's eye contact, you'll start to develop a sense of how much eye contact feels "natural." Eventually, you won't even need to consciously think about matching their eye contact – it will just happen automatically.

If you want to speed that process, there's an easy way to get a better sense of the "rhythm" of eye contact. Just watch some movies and pay attention to the eye contact given between the characters. That will help you see what kind of eye contact matching looks natural.

Bear in mind that different settings lead to different kinds of eye contact. Two flirting lovers might match eye contact shifts instantly and have more prolonged eye contact, whereas two acquaintances might take several seconds to match each other and look away often.

Also, when you analyze the movie interactions you might notice that characters will not match each other 100% – sometimes one character will look at another even though the other character is still looking away. This is totally ok.

All you need is a similar level of eye contact. There's no need to match their eye contact perfectly. If on occasion you feel like looking at them even though they're not looking at you, or you feel like looking away before they do, that's fine.

The important thing is that you are "in general" matching what they do. As long as you're in the same ballpark as them, then your eye contact will be fine. When you're starting out, you'll want to match their eye contact very closely to make sure that you stay in the safe zone.

But as you gain more experience, you'll get a better sense of what eye contact level feels natural. That will let you adjust your eye contact to what feels comfortable for both you and them, not just them.

The end result is that you won't have to think about eye contact at all – you'll just do the eye contact that feels natural for both you and your partner.

Take a bit of time to learn these good eye contact techniques, and you'll find yourself richly rewarded with more comfortable and enjoyable conversations for both you and your partners.

To Summarize:

- When your partner looks at you, look at them. When they look away, look away

- Pause for a few seconds before matching your partner's eye contact

- As you develop more experience, you won't need to match your partner's eye contact as exactly because you can rely on your instincts.

That's all there is to it!

Overcoming Anxiety: One Simple Rule

Fear often keeps us from the things we want.

Maybe we want to go talk to that guy, or ask that girl out, or go to that party. But we're afraid.

What if he doesn't want to talk to me?

What if she says no?

What if I feel awkward at the party?

In the moment, these fears can seem really big. And when our fears are big, we play it safe, which means we avoid the things we really want to do.

Fortunately, there's one simple rule you can use to give yourself courage.

10-10-10

It's called the 10-10-10 rule, and it was developed by Suzy Welch, a business writer. In a nutshell, the 10-10-10 rule asks you to imagine the likely outcomes of a decision...

- 10 minutes in the future
- 10 months in the future
- 10 years in the future

It's developed for business decisions (what will happen in 10 minutes/10 months/10 years if we launch this new product?) but it's

really useful for social situations too.

10-10-10 for Social Situations

What happens when you apply the 10-10-10 rule to social situations?

Well, let's say you're at a party and you want to strike up a conversation with someone. What are the best and worst things that might reasonably happen? Well....

- In 10 minutes, best case you will be having a great conversation, worst case the conversation will flop and you'll feel awkward.

- In 10 months, best case you are still friends with the person you talked to, worst case you have a dim memory of an awkward conversation

- In 10 years, best case you are STILL friends with the person you talked to, and there is no worst case – you're not going to remember an awkward conversation from a party ten years ago.

Long-Term Courage

When you look at it this way, the path is clear. You should start the conversation, because the potential upside (a new friend!) is much greater than the potential downside (10 minutes of awkwardness.)

And you'll find this is true in many social situations where you feel anxious or scared. When you use the 10-10-10 rule to give yourself a long-term perspective, it's much easier to overcome fear and make the best decision.

Or to put it another way – it's hard to be afraid of 10 minutes of awkwardness when you're thinking about the next 10 years of your life.

So try it out!

Next time you are afraid of taking the initiative in a social situation, just ask yourself, "If I do this, what is the best and worst thing that might reasonably happen in 10 minutes, 10 months, and 10 years?"

This only takes a moment, but it will give you a clear direction and the confidence to push past fear.

20 Seconds of Insane Courage

Growth is scary.

But growth happens one step at a time

And one little baby step, while still scary, is doable.

In the movie *We Bought A Zoo,* Matt Damon's character says that sometimes all you need is "20 seconds of insane courage."

And 20 seconds of courage, while scary, is doable.

20 Life-Changing Seconds

I don't know what 20 seconds of courage looks like for you.

But you do.

Maybe it's saying "Yes!" to that invitation. Maybe it's scheduling that first appointment with a counselor.

It might even look like taking 20 seconds to speak truth to yourself, and encourage yourself not to give up.

Regardless of what it looks like, I know you have 20 seconds of insane courage in you. You have the courage to take that next small step towards growth – even though it's scary.

So muster up your courage. Take a deep breath.

And be insanely, crazy-go-nuts brave for 20 seconds.

The Courageous Life

When you do, you'll realize two things.

First, that 20 seconds of insane bravery, while scary, is doable – and it's something that you can do again.

And second that, done often enough, 20 seconds of bravery adds up to a lifetime of courage.

Be courageous, my friends.

About the Author

I'm Dan, and I like people.

A few things about me:

• I live in Portland, Oregon and am currently pursuing a doctorate in clinical psychology.

• I spoke at TEDx about "My Life With Asperger's." You can watch my talk at http://bit.ly/tedxdan.

• I'm the author of ImproveYourSocialSkills.com, and I offer social skills coaching to clients all around the world.

Thanks again for reading the book! The support from my readers has been nothing short of amazing, and I am deeply grateful for everyone who has journeyed with me to improve their social skills.

If you have any questions or comments, feel free to get in touch. Following the example of Mr. Rogers, I respond to everyone who contacts me, so don't hesitate to reach out. You can email me at Dan@ImproveYourSocialSkills.com or at DanielWendler.com.

Made in the USA
Coppell, TX
17 September 2020

38020034R00125